Essays That Worked—
For Business Schools

Also by Curry & Kasbar

Essays That Worked:
50 Essays from Successful Applications
to the Nation's Top Colleges

Essays
THAT WORKED

FOR BUSINESS SCHOOLS

35 Essays from Successful Applications
to the Nation's Top Business Schools

Edited by
Boykin Curry and Brian Kasbar

Mustang Publishing
New Haven

Library of Congress Cataloging in Publication Data:

Essays that worked, for business schools.

　　　1. Business schools—United States—Admission.
2. Exposition (Rhetoric) 3. College applications—
United States. I. Curry, Boykin, 1966-　　　.
II. Kasbar, Brian, 1966-　　　.
HF1131E87 1987　　　808′ .066651　　　87-61082
ISBN 0-914457-19-5

10 9 8 7 6 5 4 3 2 1

Acknowledgments

This book was derived from the efforts of many students and admissions officers at some of the top business schools in America. We deeply appreciate the generosity of the applicants who gave us permission to reprint their essays and of the admissions officers who gave us their time, critiques, and advice.

We wish to extend our gratitude to three people in particular: David Weber at M.I.T.'s Sloan School, Eric Mokover at U.C.L.A., and Richard Silverman at Yale's S.O.M. They went far beyond their duties and gave us invaluable assistance. Thank you very much.

Boykin Curry
Brian Kasbar

August, 1987

For
Roosevelt Evans, Joe Beckford,
Walter A. Debboli Jr., and Bill Ohr—
men of Yale without whom this book
would not have been possible.

Table of Contents

Introduction

How important is the essay on a business school application?

"To be honest, a person's record speaks much louder to us than his essay," one admissions officer told us.

"We give it quite a bit of weight," said another.

"It's at the heart of our entire process," said someone else.

Along with your grades, your accomplishments, and, in some cases, your GMAT scores, the application essay can make the difference between acceptance and rejection. For some schools the essay is crucial. For others it will only tip the balance of a borderline candidate. After speaking with admissions officers at a number of business schools, we have tried to estimate just how important the essay can be in the admissions process.

(Of course, this graph is not exact, but it does roughly represent our understanding of the priorities of the schools.)

Irrelevant   Vital

0   5   10

Harvard

Columbia

MIT

Yale SOM

Michigan

UVA Darden

Chicago

Wharton

Stanford

UCLA

Dartmouth Tuck

Kellogg

Duke Fuqua

Over the years, each of the top business schools has developed a distinct personality. Harvard, for example, has churned out one-fifth of the major officers at Fortune 500 companies, while Yale encourages students to make a contribution to the public sector. In response to these reputations, many students become chameleons in their applications. They are executives for Harvard, math jocks for MIT, and dedicated public servants for Yale.

Of course, admission officers usually see through that ploy quickly, and even if they don't, you're probably just hurting your application when you try to apply as someone you're not. Inconsistencies between your essays and your record are easy to spot; sentiment and expertise are tough to fake. The brochures for several business schools stress "general management," and one admissions officer told us that he is flooded with essays using the term "general manager" over and over in obsequious attempts to win a place. "It can become so repetitive," he said, "that I can't help but question the candidate's sincerity. The term has become meaningless."

Obviously, you should emphasize the parts of your personality and record which coincide with the school's interests. But avoid overdoing it. Be selective, but be yourself—it's the best sales pitch you can make.

In our previous book on undergraduate application essays, we discussed what kinds of content and tone were most appropriate in applying to college. Much of our advice holds true for business schools as well.

The overwhelming complaint from undergraduate admissions officers was that reading 13,000 essays on the same few topics in a span of three months is a mind-numbing experience. Most essays are dry and overwritten. They are often "corrected" by so many friends and relatives that the life gets sucked out. One undergraduate admissions officer explained that "few applicants understand what we want to read, and they rarely go out on a limb to be witty or controversial." Anxious applicants become so afraid of saying the wrong thing that they end up saying nothing. Such sterilization can mean unbearable monotony for the hapless admissions staff, so don't treat your essay like a psychological minefield. What seems "safe" to you is probably deadly boring to a weary admissions officer.

The officer at one top school resorts to dramatic measures to combat essay fatigue. "I try to change the scenery when I read essays," he said. "I read them in the park or out on my boat. You know what? Even that doesn't help."

You can imagine, then, the impact that a lively, original essay can have. For starters, you are *noticed*, and that's much of the battle. But also, you have done a favor for the tired reader—and favors are often returned.

After reading the essays in this book, we hope you will understand better the boundaries of tone and content within which you can work, and we hope you see how large the boundaries are. Since these essays represent some of the best writing out of thousands of pieces submitted each year, they should inspire your creativity and help you feel more comfortable about the admissions process. As the essays demonstrate, you can be exciting and natural without resorting to outrageous gimmicks or immature poses. An accurate, enthusiastic reflection of your personality can make for a refreshing—and we hope successful—essay. Good luck!

An Interview
With an Admissions Officer

Although different schools attach different levels of importance to the application essays, and although each school may be looking for a slightly different type of student, admissions officers have surprisingly similar desires. They want brevity. They want sincerity. They want mature enthusiasm. And a little humor—when it's truly humorous—doesn't hurt.

But as we perused the application questions and tried to compose our own answers, we found ourselves asking a number of questions. How "business-like" should we be? How much can we joke around? Can we relax and be the readers' chum, or should we treat them like clients? Should we tell them what they want to hear, or should we be totally honest, even at the risk of being boring?

We asked these and other questions to dozens of admissions officers at almost every major business school in the country. The following is a condensed version of those interviews:

What's the difference between application essays for business school and the essays we wrote to get into college?
The main difference is the way the author presents himself. What we ask of a college graduate is much more difficult than what colleges ask of a high-school senior. And it should be. We don't want applicants to simply give a self-absorbed description of themselves, like they did for their college application. Rather, we want them to describe the world they see around them, and their place in it. An analogy we like to use around here is that with the essay, a student fashions a lens for us to view the world. From looking at the quality of that lens, we hope to judge the quality of its maker.

When we finish an essay, we expect to have learned something about the applicant and an industry or management or business. If an applicant has worked in a steel plant, for example, it should be interesting to see his understanding of the problems in the industry. What kind of management problems has he observed, and how would he change things? You can't expect that type of analysis from undergraduates.

We also expect more maturity for business school. That's partly a function of age—we're often dealing with people in their late 20's or 30's—but it's also an issue of direction. Undergraduates are coming to school to explore. It's hard to justify giving one of a few MBA spots to someone who is not pretty committed to a business career.

Do you want a description of a person or just his accomplishments?
We want an essay that brings the whole set of numbers into a coherent form. We want inconsistencies explained, and we want to see diverse activities as different facets of a single personality. We'd like to be able to say, "Oh, he did that, yeah, that makes sense. That fits with what we have." Both the performer and his track record should be discussed, so that we can know the person underneath all the accomplishments, and also how those activities affected that person.

An applicant could discuss, for example, how his jobs at a computer firm and at a wholesale food distributor will help him make grocery stores more efficient. Or how working in a defense firm led him to see the need for military procurement reforms.

Are there any hackneyed topics that applicants should avoid?
I would be lying if I said we dive enthusiastically into the drama of every investment banker's grueling program, but most of our questions are very personalized and no two people have exactly the same experience. Since we ask fairly specific questions, most answers are in the same vein, but we still get a good mix of ideas.

The similarity in topics is not what makes essays dull—and most of them certainly are. It's the monotonous style. Applicants tend to use too many big words and amorphous adjectives and not enough colorful details and observations.

If reading thousands of these essays is so boring, would you prefer that applicants try to entertain you?
First off, let me say that gimmicks do *not* work. This year we got an essay written in crayon on construction paper. It really hurt the applicant because it made us question his maturity and competence. That kind of joking might work occasionally for a college application, but we are

dealing with much more sophisticated people at this level. Jokers are admitted only if their credentials are so good that we just can't refuse them.

You do have to captivate the reader somewhat, but many people hurt themselves by going too far. One applicant wrote an eight-page essay when we asked for one page. He was entertaining, but he didn't arrive at any point. And he didn't get very far in the admissions process, either. It's like marketing: get our attention and then *say something*. Just grabbing notice isn't enough.

I loathe 'cute' essays. Nothing bugs me more than someone trying to be my funny pal. Dry wit is good, but when someone starts off with "Wow, investment banking is so neat," I just cringe.

I suppose my best advice is to write a mature essay—nothing too formal, though—and to integrate your personality into it as best you can. Don't be afraid to say what you feel. Remember that serious is not synonymous with humorless. We love wit, but it has to be backed up with meaningful points.

What about the off-beat essay? Does it have an advantage because it grabs your attention?

It's true that I get tired of the same self-descriptions of the thousands of people who apply here each year. We could fill our class ten times over with people from Wall Street, and it would be nice to see someone who is a bit 'off-beat.' Given comparable work experience and success, I'd much rather take someone who has run a farm in Iowa than an investment banker.

But being off-beat just to get attention won't work. The uniqueness has to mesh with the rest of the application. We *do* want to see different facets of an applicant's personality. We *do* want people to show us how they differ from the other 7,000 applicants. But different doesn't mean outrageous. It can mean a New York consultant who takes ghetto kids camping on weekends, or a computer whiz with a passion for scuba diving. It does not mean some goofball just trying to impress us with a bunch of one-liners.

What advantage does a good writer have? Does style beat substance?

We try to be sensitive to poor writing skills, because we aren't looking for future authors or even scholars, necessarily. We're looking for future business leaders. We realize that engineers will be at a disadvantage when compared to advertisers, and we take that into account when we read the essays. But there's no question that writing style does make a difference. A good writer is convincing and engaging. She knows how to intrigue an audience, and she backs up her points with specific examples. Her ideas flow smoothly, and she makes the reader's job a lot easier. And if she is intelligent and witty, her essay is hard to forget.

Unfortunately, we get few essays of that caliber each year, and we won't hold it against you if you don't write a literary masterpiece. But we also keep in mind that skillful presentation and communication are crucial aspects of business.

If your readers want a good piece of advice when they start writing, let me say this: relax and just write. Only a small percentage of people bowl us over with style. What we really want is content.

One applicant wrote an essay wondering why people on death row always ask for a cigarette instead of writing down something about their lives or even making a last statement. Well, it's incredibly hard to express yourself, and we know that, so don't let your anxiety about style interfere with your need to write a meaningful essay.

So what are you looking for?
An honest, thoughtful essay. I know that sounds a little trite, but it's something we rarely see. Not only is that the best essay to read, but it should be the easiest to write. Concocting ridiculous anecdotes, attention-getting schemes, or a fictitious portrait is really a big waste of time and energy.

We want people to be vibrant, but we don't want gimmicks. We want a business-like approach, but we don't want to be fed dull, pompous lines.

Everyone wants us to give a recipe and a roadmap to the process, but what we want is someone who can navigate his own course. Within guidelines, of course.

Some Sample Questions

The following are questions from a few recent business school applications. Bear in mind that most of these schools require you to answer four or five questions.

From Wharton:
Why did you decide to pursue graduate management education? Looking ahead, what type of job would you expect or like to have five **and** ten years after receiving your master's degree? What is your ultimate career objective? In realizing these goals, do you foresee your career as a business leader having an impact on society at large?

What do you consider to have been your single most significant achievement to date?

From Kellogg:
What is the most challenging problem that you have faced, and how have you solved it?

From Stanford:
Describe an ethical dilemma that you have personally encountered. What alternative actions did you consider and why? Do **not** tell us what you decided to do.

From the Univ. of Michigan:
There is a lot of controversy over the usefulness of the MBA. What do you consider to be the strengths and weaknesses of the degree?

From Dartmouth:
What are your principal interests outside of your job or school? Why do they appeal to you?

From Harvard:
Given your experience with your current employer (or school you attend) and given the opportunity to effect one change, what would that be? How would you implement the change?

Discuss the vocations or professions, other than administration, which you may have seriously considered.

From M.I.T.'s Sloan School:
The statement of objectives is your opportunity to describe your reasons for wanting to do graduate work in management at the Sloan School. . . We have not posed specific questions for you, preferring that you determine which aspects of your background and aspirations are relevant to your application.

From UCLA:
Write your own essay question and answer it. Take a risk.

The Essays

For organizational purposes, we divided the essays into seven groups: Essays That Discuss Strengths and Weaknesses, Ethical Essays, Essays About Work Experiences, Essays About the MBA, Essays About Accomplishments, Extracurricular Essays, and Off-Beat Essays. Please understand that this grouping is totally artificial. You don't have to write an essay that would fit neatly into one of these catagories.

We created the introductions to each grouping based on our own research and on comments submitted by admissions officers when they sent us the essays. As well as being a fine piece of writing, an essay might also exemplify a "type." For example, the "N•TROPY" piece is a good example of the Extracurricular Essay. So, if you are going to write this type of essay, pay close attention to the advice in the group's introduction, as well as to the actual essay.

Of course, the essay question will probably limit your range of responses. When you applied to college, you most likely had a vague, open-ended topic, like "Write a brief essay that describes who you are." But graduate school topics tend to be fairly specific, like the UCLA application which said, "Discuss two or three situations in the past three years where you have taken a leadership role. How do these events demonstrate your managerial potential?" Although your answer to a topic like that must be tightly structured, you still have a great opportunity to present a unique and memorable image.

The essays that follow are reproduced exactly as they were submitted, though of course the typeface and spacing are different. We did not correct punctuation, spelling, or grammar errors in the essays. But note that rarely would such correction be needed.

Since the authors of all the essays requested anonymity, we have deleted proper names and sometimes substituted a more general name in place of a specific reference. In addition, at the request of a few schools, we sometimes disguised the name of the school to which the writer applied. However, our substitutions never distort the content of the essay.

Finally, a warning. We know that no one would be foolish enough to copy one of these essays verbatim. However, we realize that some readers might be tempted to take an essay and "change it around" to suit his application. We hope you know how incredibly stupid that would be. For one thing, stealing an idea from an essay in this book or "paraphrasing" it would be dishonest—and maybe even a criminal violation of copyright. For another thing, it would severely jeopardize your chance of getting into a business school. Most admissions officers have read this book, and none would ever admit a plagiarist.

The following pages demonstrate the creative potential of the business school application essay. We hope they will give you the confidence to write a bold, personal piece that will show an admissions committee why you're special. Enjoy these essays, study them, and let them be a catalyst for your own creativity.

Essays That Discuss
Strengths and Weaknesses

A common essay theme concerns your strengths and weaknesses. This topic can be a proxy for many subtler questions: Are you arrogant? Do you lack self-confidence? Do you understand yourself? Or do you just *think* you do? Are you honest and straightforward, or a little too shrewd and manipulative?

A common response among successful writers is to offer a broad but observable strength backed by anecdotal evidence. Colorful examples which illustrate your strengths can be quite engaging, and they allow you to make your point strongly without bragging. But watch out if you find yourself using a lot of adjectives and just a few verbs. No one wants someone who talks a lot and acts a little. If you have many strengths, make sure you are *exhibiting* them and not just describing them.

Analytic ability and interpersonal skills are essential to business and life. Be sure to demonstrate some talent in these areas.

In the weaknesses department, we observed an interesting trend. The best weaknesses were usually strengths in disguise. "I work too hard" is a common refrain. "I'm impatient with those less intelligent than myself" is another. While these "positive weaknesses" are often legitimate and require attention, they are usually just strengths in excess. Such "weaknesses" can tag a writer as insincere and sly.

But not one successful essay we read described a weakness of character, motivation, or intelligence, such as: "I lie sometimes," "I get bored at work," or "I have trouble keeping up." Recent studies of high-level business people reveal that many feel like frauds, that they believe they hold positions they don't really deserve. Among successful applicants, however, this type of weakness is rarely discussed.

We're not telling you to hold back the truth and make up some contrived essay. If your grades are mediocre, don't say you are "too driven" at school. But this is one question where you simply have to be sensitive. Would Harvard rather spend resources on someone who is "always late to work" or someone who is a self-proclaimed "workaholic"? All things being equal, the workaholic will win.

With effort, you can discuss real weaknesses without sounding bitter or pathetic. Think about yourself for a few days. Spend an hour writing out stories that show your faults. Don't be inhibited or strategic. Be brutal. This exercise is interesting and not too painful, and it will give you an accurate, honest foundation for your essay.

Then be discrete.

What is your greatest weakness? Here is a sample of the brutal, wrenching self-criticism found in a few essays. Bear in mind that most admissions officers file such phrases in the Give-Me-a-Break Dept.

My greatest weakness is
". . .my tendency to over-research topics when time is available."
". . .my desire to excel."
". . .that I do not like to waste time."
". . .that I expect as much out of others as I do out of myself."
". . .that sometimes people confuse what I have to say to them."
". . .that I'm too much of a leader."

Motivation and creativity are two strengths I could contribute to the community at [your business school]. As my academic and employment histories will attest, I am an extremely motivated individual. As an undergraduate, I enrolled in extra units and graduated a semester early. As a professional, I advanced from a light staff to a heavy staff nine months ahead of the normal progression, and I attribute this demonstration of drive and energy as the primary factor in securing employment as a management consultant. Regarding creativity, the problem solving orientation of consulting requires a high degree of creativity and imagination. I have demonstrated my abilities by creating new and unique approaches and solutions.

A characteristic I am attempting to improve is my self-confidence. As a new consultant, I have tried to overcome the credibility barrier to develop the effective interchange necessary to provide quality counsel. The task has proven to be difficult. Working with associates holding MBA's from the top business schools and advising senior executives with more business experience than my age is unnerving. However, the interaction demanded [by your] case method will, without doubt, build my self-esteem and confidence.

The attribute that has contributed most to my career as a journalist is my ability to analyze complex and fast-changing situations, no matter how unfamiliar or specialized the subject matter. Because of my reputation for quick learning and flexibility, I often have been assigned by my editors to cover emergency situations and complicated subject matters—from corporate takeovers and complex investigative stories, to natural disasters and guerrilla warfare. And I have repeatedly proven my ability to cover these stories under the extreme competitive pressures of a daily newspaper.

I have learned to spot key trends amid masses of seemingly unrelated information. My employer demands analytical and thoughtful coverage from its reporters, forcing me to look beyond superficial news events to find the underlying causes or to predict future developments.

An important tool in this process is my ability to communicate. Obviously, my ability to express myself in writing has been vital. Just as important, however, is the skill in personal communications I have developed to cajole information from reluctant news sources or negotiate my way through hazardous situations. While relentless in fulfilling my responsibilities to gather information, I believe I know how to do so without falling prey to the over-aggressiveness often ascribed to journalists.

And, to present controversies in a balanced manner, I've relied on my natural ability to get along with a wide variety of news sources. I have learned to delve into the motivations of people totally unlike myself, putting aside my own biases to absorb the views of others. At the same time, when the facts support harsh judgements and conclusions, I have been willing to withstand extreme pressures and criticism that result from controversial articles.

Moreover, I've proven adept at working by myself for extended periods of time and then blending easily into teams of reporters and editors. On several occasions I've been assigned to team projects because of my ability to help coordinate groups of highly individual journalists who otherwise couldn't, or wouldn't, work together.

A weakness I've worked to correct is my tendency to over-research topics when I have the time available. I have occasionally let my natural curiosity, and my drive to ensure that I have adequate information to support my published conclusions, lead me too deeply into research projects. I have recognized this problem, however; I believe my accomplishments show that for the most part I have been able to balance the need to work efficiently with my responsibility to thoroughly report information for my stories.

If I were to read this application as an admissions officer, my greatest concern about the individual in question would be a depth of character and experience that might not yet have developed in a person of my age. Whenever I read a resume or application of a young "fast track" professional, I question the one-dimensionality that all too frequently characterizes bright, ambitious but otherwise shallow achievers. Were I involved in the admissions process, I would make every effort to admit individuals who are highly motivated, and performance-oriented; that fact notwithstanding, however, I would also seek those individuals who possess the intangible yet compelling personal attributes that are distilled from a wealth of tangibly unique experiences.

After an in-depth reading of this application, I form a mental image of a 24 year-old, bright, inquisitive challenge-seeker who possesses a natural bent for the appreciation of foreign cultures and a fascination with global issues. At an age where none of the truly formidable crossroads of life have yet been met, might not this person expand her intellectual horizons in a more unrestricted manner, for example, by apprenticing as a wine-taster in one of the great french wine chateaux? Or studying art history and language at the Sorbonne? Or even experimenting with hidden talents at the culinary schools of La Varenne or La Notre in Paris? Why isn't this applicant studying political science in an Eastern Bloc university, journeying by train across Russia, sailing up the Yellow River on a barge excursion or trekking through the Himalayas of Nepal? For a

motivated, resourceful individual, the scope of uniquely
enriching cultural opportunities is unlimited: archaeological
digs in the Andes, rough water sailing off Australia, an internship on the Senate Foreign Affairs Committee, or set design for
a theater on Broadway. It is evident that the individual
described herein possesses a surfeit of qualifications, talent and
practical experience. In the final analysis, however, the question
is one of whether the individual also possesses the diversity of
lessons, both the everyday and the unusual, the exciting and
the mundane, that ordinary life (in many not-so-ordinary places)
has to offer.

Why do I believe that you will overrule the consideration expressed in this essay? The answer is the following: I believe
that an individual who realizes the need for depth of character
forged by unrestricted intellectual exploration is a long way
along the road to acquiring that sought-after depth. And I am
enough of an optimist to believe that I can juggle business
school and a concurrent diversity of experiences that will allow
me to progress the rest of the way down that road.

My mother is a Buddhist; my father, a Baptist. My mother was the only daughter of a wealthy elite Korean family who gave her the best of all the social and educational advantages. My father was the fifth son of a poor uneducated family from Virginia who sent him on his way to work for the U.S. Army in Korea. When my mother married my father, she was completely disinherited and was never allowed to see her family again. The legacy of difficult choices and the blending of two diverse cultures have had a unique impact on my character and my perspective on life.

I made a choice at an early age to be strong. When I was seven months old, I contacted a virus which the local Korean doctor diagnosed as flu. It turned out to be polio. From the example set by my mother to marry my father despite all odds, I realized that I too could accomplish anything I wanted to do in life. Thus, I have developed a reservoir of enormous inner strength. I set high standards for myself and I am, perhaps, tougher on myself than anyone else. Having polio is like having a ready-made excuse for any failure. I made the choice not to believe in excuses.

Because of my determination to succeed, I have been enthusiastic about life and all that it has to offer. I am curious, open-minded, adventuresome, and somewhat daring. While in Korea, I was the President of the Junior Travel and Culture Club and I organized trips throughout Korea and Japan. I have ventured into the depths of majestic, multi-colored caves and I have hiked up mountains to see Buddhist statues carved into stone walls. I have even led a group of students to Panmunjum, the military demarcation of North and South Korea. I once stepped over the boundary into North Korea only to be suddenly circled by twelve well-armed North Korean guards. I told them that I was just testing them out.

As a student leader and a collegiate debator at USC, I have traveled extensively throughout the United States. Many times I have competed at debate tournaments during winter in the east coast or in the mid-west. It may have taken me longer to get my briefcases to the next debate round while plowing through several inches of snow, but I had the distinct advantage of having more time to think about my debate strategy. When I traveled to Washington, D.C. to speak out on financial aid and tuition issues, other students leaders remembered me and I was able to successfully organize a national letter-writing campaign against the proposed federal financial aid cuts.

Initiative and independence have characterized my life. My family moved to a rural farming community atop the Ozark Mountains when I was 16 years old. There were more cows than people there. I knew that I wasn't meant to be Rebecca of Sunnybrook Farm so when I graduated from high school, I moved to San Francisco and found an apartment and a job on my own. It was this same independence that has compelled me to finance my undergraduate education by winning several scholarships and working full- and part-time during school.

I am continually learning to balance my fierce independence with my strong belief in the worth of others. Having lived in such diverse places as Seoul (Korea), Arkansas, San Francisco, and Los Angeles, I have come to appreciate the differences and similarities among seemingly incompatible cultures. I am perceptive and sensitive. Perhaps this is the result of the skills I had to develop at an early age. As a child, I quickly learned that people did not necessarily mean what they said. Ironically, instead of being helped by others, I found myself in a role of making others comfortable relating to a child who had polio.

The synthesis of my unique background and my understanding of other people has resulted in others perceiving me to be a leader with a tremendous amount of energy, perserverence, and integrity. People believe in me. At USC, I convinced the student government to take tough stands on academic standards and to fight for more student services. I am most comfortable in a leadership position, and at the same time, I must balance this with my belief in teamwork. I don't want to be so strong that I subjugate the weak; rather, I want to inspire others to be strong. When I believe in something, I am passionate, enthusiastic, and driven. I have the ability to communicate this belief and commitment to others to an extent that both surprises and humbles me.

I believe I communicate effectively with small and large groups. While [a member of the student government] at USC, I especially enjoyed making presentations and speeches before student groups, administrators, and the Faculty Senate. I had the reputation of being able to move a crowd to tears, although this always seemed to happen when I told a joke.

Debating has further sharpened my verbal and analytical skills. I have learned to think on my feet, to defend a position, and to attack cases. I remember one particular round in which my partner and I were debating a team of young men from an eastern school. Their opening arguments ended with innuendos about the inadequacy of women to debate. Aside from being an ad hominem argument, I realized that it was a personal attack since there are very few female collegiate debators. I looked at my partner and said, "Let's kill 'em." We did.

I am learning to evaluate whether I would like to debate or to persuade. I have won more arguments on a personal level by weakening my position, yet I have the ability, and many times desire, to over-kill an argument. I want to learn to become passionate about the right issues and to distinguish those from irrelevant ones.

My strengths have developed out of my weaknesses and my weaknesses may come out of my strengths. Weaknesses many times results from not knowing when to subdue strengths. I am learning to achieve a balance between the two. By synthesizing my skills, I am increasing the range of strengths that I can use in appropriate circumstances. As a manager, this is important for I know there will be a time to speak out and a time to listen, a time to lead and a time to follow, and a time to be confident and a time to be humble.

My greatest weakness lies in my desire to excel. I set goals for myself which I expect to attain. Falling short of my goals results in the growth of my determination to succeed. Because of my desire to excel, I often believe that a finished product which I have produced is flawless; therefore, outside criticism, although greatly appreciated, is rarely integrated into a revised form. Another major weakness lies in my desire to direct whatever situation I am involved in. I feel that if I am interested enough in the situation to be involved, then I am probably the most capable in the group of directing it successfully toward its ultimate goal. The inability to lead would result in boredom; for I am easily bored when lacking a challenging endeavor or an invigorating environment. In summary, my need and obsession to excel at every task is what I recognize as my major weakness.

Giving an evaluation of yourself is always difficult, but I believe those people that are candid about themselves and truly understand their strengths and weaknesses will be the most successful. My two greatest strengths are self confidence, and determination. I do not believe in negative thinking, and am confident that I can accomplish whatever I set my mind to. I am ambitious, and believe I am a natural leader through my ability to express myself and organize people and things. I like to be given responsibility because I believe I have good judgement, and I like to make decisions quickly.

My weaknesses are in large part connected to my strengths. My most glaring weakness is my impatience. I am a person who does not like to waste time, nor do I like to wait. My impatience sometimes gets me in trouble with people when they are slower at performing a task than I. I often find myself apologizing in these situations. Another weakness of mine is that I am occasionally too bossy. Often when I am involved in an activity I will try to take up a leadership role and delegate responsibility, which sometimes unnerves people. I do not do this purposely, but I frequently am able to analyze a situation quicker than most, and then I act on impulse. My last weakness is that I can seem overbearing. When I go full steam into a project I want everyone around me to share my enthusiasm for that project. If they do not, they may find my zest to get the project completed abrasive or overbearing.

Ethical Essays

In the age of Ivan Boesky and the materialistic yuppie, business schools are increasingly concerned about the ethical standards of the leaders they will graduate. Many applications now require students to discuss an ethical dilemma, and these essays can be tougher than you think.

Don't congratulate yourself for being *always* honest, because, honestly, you're not. White lies are a part of everyone's social routine. If you glibly write "I never lie," you will reveal more about your personality than you realize. On the other hand, don't cynically ponder how easy it would be to have taken "the other route." Such a tack makes you at the least a martyr and at the worst a potential criminal.

Instead, approach the ethical essay with honest realism. Write briefly about the responsibilities you believe in, and then discuss how you have upheld certain principles. You need to show that, as an intelligent, educated person, you are willing to pay a price for high ethical standards. But be careful not to overdo it, because hokey insincerity is obvious and devastating. Discuss something you truly care about, even if your story is not so dramatic as those in this group.

And don't write about problems that you created for yourself. White-collar wheedling like expense-account padding and insider trading should not be problems. But whether you should turn in a fellow employee for his misconduct is sometimes a very tough decision.

The most effective ethical essays involve a specific situation that sheds light on the difficult moral choices we all face from time to time. While you don't always have to present The Answer to a big problem, you do need to show the admissions officer how you handle and how you think about ethical dilemmas.

I experienced an ethical dilemma in conjunction with a litigation consulting assignment. In 1984, [my company] was engaged by a national law firm to design and perform a study measuring the effects of divestiture on working capital for [two corporations]. In short, $289 million was in dispute, and the findings of our study would help resolve the case before the arbitration panel.

For seventeen months, [the consultants] worked to deliver preliminary conclusions. To support the preliminary findings, and thus finalize the engagement, I was assigned to the project and delegated responsibility for the payroll section, one of twelve subject areas under consideration. I had three months to perform a limited review, to analyze the computer payroll system, to summarize the findings, and to prepare a conclusion to be presented before the arbitrators.

Seven weeks into the project, I uncovered a flaw in a payroll methodology which wrongfully benefited [one corporation] by $ .7 million. I immediately conveyed this error to the project manager, but he was unreceptive to any change. Correcting the methodology would impact other subject areas, thus requiring an additional 200 hours of fieldwork. Furthermore, he reasoned the net error was immaterial in relation to the total in question, and any major methodological change occurring in these later stages would cast doubt on the preliminary findings. Dissatisfied with the disposition, I brought the matter to the attention of the project senior manager. I agreed completely that the error was small. Nonetheless, it was a mistake. To jeopardize the reputation of [the company] seemed irrational. To emphasize my position on the matter, I stated I could not provide expert testimony unless a change in methodology transpired. Fortunately, the senior manager accepted my reasoning, and my recommendations for change were adopted.

About four years ago I recognized that my father had become an alcoholic. My father didn't understand the problem; he couldn't understand anything. I was eventually faced with an ethical dilemma on how to manage an alcoholic father.

Alcoholism is a devastating disease. It can destroy its victim and cripple all of the victim's friends and family. Over the years I had cautioned my father on the peril of his increased drinking, but neither patient pleas nor harsh lectures had any effect. Problem drinker, alcoholic, drunk—eventually all the words conjured up the horrible picture of an extraordinary man giving up everything to wallow in a stupor. My family read books on the subject. We consulted doctors. We sent my father to a rehabilitation center. Nothing helped.

Finally, his psychiatrist recommended as a final course of action that we desert my father. The doctor argued that, forced to face the problem alone, my father might find the will to recover—or die. Without a drastic turnaround, death was an increasingly imminent fate, and, meanwhile, he was dragging the entire family down with him.

The ethical conflict which I faced consumed me. The doctor offered a gambit to save my father; yet how could I leave my father while still loving him?

A few months ago I was faced with a situation on my job that proved to be quite an ethical dilemma. The company I work for is a major government contractor that handles several contracts at once. The government assigns a certain amount of money to be spent on each project handled by the company. All labor and materials used to complete the project are charged to the pre-assigned allocated contract accounts. A specific set of contract numbers are used when materials and labor are consumed. These contract numbers are used for accounting purposes, as the government mandates that all materials and labor consumed be itemized by the contract to which they apply. The government explicitly prohibits using specific contract numbers on other projects than those that have already been assigned by contract agreement. If a project needs more funding, the company must renegotiate their contract with the government, and not take money from programs that have adequate funds.

One of my projects ran into some difficulties, and as a result the projected production schedule deadlines became in jeopardy. To speed up the production would require more labor and materials, and consequently, more money. A problem resulted because there was simply not enough money available to fulfill the contractual obligations in a timely fashion. Due to the deadline pressure, my immediate supervisor instructed me to assign all my labor, material procurements, rework orders and rekits of assemblies to contracts that were not related to the work I was performing on. I informed him that the proper procedure was to simply request more government funding for the project through the Program Management Office.

I had recently read where General Dynamics was found guilty of similar practices that my boss was strongly advising me to perform. When I told him that I believed that taking such action was improper, he told me that this situation would last for only a short period of time. My immediate reaction was displeasure. I knew he was asking me to perform a duty that was unethical, not to mention illegal. An additional problem was that my supervisor and I had become very good friends. Despite our friendship, I felt he was unethically using his responsibilities, and to ask me to aid him confronted my personal integrity. He told me to try to understand the problems we were encountering in order to meet contract dates. With time, we could receive additional funding to complete contract. In the mean time, in order to keep the production moving, he wanted to use other program's accounts to continue production on our contract.

After giving the situation considerable thought, I brought the matter to the attention of our manager, who consequently relieved my supervisor of his duties.

There were several reasons that prompted me to report my supervisor. First, his proposed actions were illegal. I was positive my supervisor was aware of the consequences of his actions and the incredible dilemma he was putting me in. The entire company was cognizant of the General Dynamics case and its effect. I could have been fired, or the company could have been subjected to severe penalties. I take my responsibilities as an employee seriously. I enjoy the feeling of being part of a productive team, working together to achieve a common goal. The actions contemplated by my supervisor was disruptive of this team concept, and would no doubt result in counter-productive activity.

Secondly, if I complied with my supervisor's request, I never know if he would have asked me to perform another unethical or illegal task. I value my personal integrity and moral obligations more than friendship.

This experience taught me the importance of moral integrity and teamwork. In order to have any successful enterprise you need a group of workers that possess high standards. If you do not have this integrity, there will be indecisiveness among workers, with some workers benefiting from their dishonesty and others feeling resentment over dishonest co-workers gain.

Only by having a common goal and common means of achieving that goal can an enterprise hope for success. My supervisor did not share the goals and moral responsibilities of the company. His actions were potentially disruptive and destructive. Being committed to both integrity and success, I was left with no other option but to report him.

Essays About Work Experiences

Unlike most graduate schools, business schools prefer students with some work experience. Nothing speaks louder in business than past business. A few good years on Wall Street—or in a factory—can sometimes supplant a lifetime of mediocre grades.

How quickly did you learn on the job? How did you develop? Did you seize initiative or did you punch the clock from nine to five? Did you gain insights into the industry as a whole, or did you become a master of your little routine?

Work experience can mean a lot of things besides pushing paper at the office, and we found admissions officers yearning for a wider range of topics and perspectives. Reporters, politicians, and PTA presidents can display skills that are vital in other professions. And unconventional jobs and experiences are often more vivid and interesting to read about than the standard two-year stint at a bank.

And don't believe the common myth that the Ivy Leaguers who get into the plum training courses on Wall Street have an edge. You don't have to toil for Salomon Brothers to know about serious work. Harvard has even released a list ranking investment banking at the *bottom* of their "desired experience" list.

All of the essays in this group make a good story. Each has an introduction, conflict, and a resolution. Each story reveals something about the writer's personality and attitude. Business schools don't want your resume or "One Day in the Life of a Consultant." They already know that stuff. They want to know what *you* brought to a job that made you different, interesting, and more effective. Yes, you may have the endurance to make good grades at Princeton or number-crunch at MIT. But are you creative and open-minded, too?

Late last year, election in [my town] led to a major disruption in my standard modus operandi on the Council. Prior to the election, I had served the role of an unofficial majority leader in a rather philosophically-divided Council. In the split of liberals vs. left-of-liberals, I led the liberal faction.

However, last November, after being unable to find a strong candidate for the vacant seat on our five member city council, I found myself suddenly in the minority. Depression gripped me for a couple of weeks; after all, I had so many plans for our still new city, and now they all appeared dashed. Furthermore, I had previously been offered the mayorship by my colleagues on three occassions, and now when I was finally prepared to take it in anticipation of my re-election, I no longer had the guaranteed votes with which to do it.

Not being a quitter, I couldn't throw the towel in, so I sat back and developed a strategy. Although able to command only two votes on many issues of significant importance that were coming up on the Council agenda, I began to find new ways to accomplish my goals. I have learned to bring new forces to bear on issues, including organizing the community behind my position, depoliticizing previously controversial issues, and generally breaking my colleagues voting block. This has not been easy and requires a large time investment. However, by playing off their differences and each one's desire to be the leader, I have had some successes.

The key I find is to not act like I am part of a minority. By approaching an issue from an appearance of strength, and with a superior command of the issues being debated, I am frequently able to protect my interests and accomplish what I promised my constituents. And on those occasions where I know the battle is lost, I spend extensive amounts of time with city staff assuring that even though I am going to lose I have excluded the worst possible scenarios.

Although I may not always be on the winning side of an issue now, I have succeeded in containing the damage wrought by the shift in council majorities. Beyond this, I have also been successful in publicly securing the unanimous commitment of my colleagues to elect me to the post of Mayor this spring, as well as received the public endorsements of both major political organizations in [my town] for my election next year.

After diligent review I am prepared to begin a career as a real estate developer. The reasons for this decision are many.

My involvement with the real estate industry began at an early age. My father, son of an Italian immigrant, pursued his father's occupation as a carpenter. He successfully renovated several buildings in the New Haven area, converting their use to rental apartments, and with the assistance of my mother actively managed these properties. Each summer from 1970 to 1982, I worked with my father and two brothers in this family endeavor. During this period, I was exposed to several aspects of residential real estate, including the construction and renovation of buildings, the maintenance of existing properties, and the marketing of units to new tenants. At eighteen, although I was qualified to work in the construction trades, I was fortunate to be among the first generation of my family to pursue a college education.

I chose to attend the University of Pennsylvania to integrate a thorough liberal arts education with a B.S. in Economics at the Wharton School. At Penn I maintained a healthy balance between academic studies, athletics, and social activities. Through competition on the lightweight crew team, several semesters of rugby, and as an active member of my fraternity, I learned the importance of team work and leadership in achieving a common goal. I hope to bring this spirit of competition and team effort to your school and my fellow students.

To combine the strong analytical skills I developed at Penn with my background in real estate, I chose a position as a financial analyst with [a real estate finance firm on] Wall Street. This group of twenty professionals was formed in 1982 and has since acquired over $2.2 billion in income-producing properties for clients. I was initially hired for the two year analyst program, but have since been promoted to the associate level and asked to stay with the firm. I am currently involved in all aspects of acquiring investment-grade real estate.

In order to acquire quality assets at favorable costs our firm has been funding projects at early stages of development. Through my increasing participation with real estate developers in these joint ventures, I have become intrigued with the critical role they play in shaping our environment. The developer is a person of many talents who exercises both imagination and skill in a variety of disciplines from design, planning, law, construction, management, finance and marketing. In comparing this role with the specialized role I am currently playing in the industry, I realize that it is as a developer that I will best be able to realize my potential. I have decided to step back, analyze the situation, and take the necessary steps toward realizing this goal.

In collaboration with my brother, who is currently studying architecture in Boston, I plan to form a real estate development group that will emphasize projects of functional design which provide a social benefit. We will construct affordable housing through the rehabilitation of existing under-utilized urban structures (i.e. warehouses, mill buildings, abandoned housing). With our family background in renovation we will provide quality housing at costs substantially below new construction, while revitalizing decaying urban neighborhoods.

To begin this endeavor, I have recently purchased a three-story vacant brick building in the changing Boston neighborhood of Charlestown. I am currently negotiating a construction loan with a local bank and will occupy the building in February. With my brother as architect, I will extensively renovate the structure into residential units by the summer. I anticipate renting the lower two floors, covering my mortgage, and living free and clear on the top floor as I pursue other opportunities and my graduate education.

Expanding this concept on a larger scale, however, will require more formal training. In pursuing this goal, several aspects of your program appeal to me. The small size allows for graduate study on a more human scale, while its use of various teaching methods provide a more lively, effective approach to learning. More important, are the additional resources available throughout the institute. . .

Your program will provide me with the flexibility to pursue a general management curriculum to acquire the knowledge and skills fundamental to managerial decision-making. I expect to specialize in corporate strategy and policy to help formulate and implement a viable business plan for my entrepreneurial endeavor. To this I would combine a study of the current trends in finance, to raise capital in today's increasingly sophisticated market place.

The management skills I will learn together with my prior experience and education will allow me to realize my goal of forming and operating a successful real estate organization which will have a positive impact in shaping our environment.

My investment bank's internal system for the allocation of revenues and expenses among divisions produces a competitive, uncooperative relationship between investment banking and sales and trading that has resulted in the loss of business and market share for the firm. Currently, the expense for developing a product is allocated to the division making the expenditure. Revenues are allocated equally between the Investment Banking Division and a sales and trading division (i.e., Equity or Fixed Income Divisions), if employees from both divisions are involved in the transaction. An employee is then allocated revenues from his division. Since the year-end bonus, which comprises the largest portion of yearly compensation, is determined principally on an individual's net revenue, the internal accounting system sets the guidelines for working relationships within the firm.

The results of the accounting system are a stifled product development effort and poor information flow between divisions. After expensing the development of a product, a group greedily hoards its new possession to assure that somebody else does not reap the fruits of its labor without remunerating the originator of the product. Frequently, therefore, product development efforts are duplicated. Similarly, as an example, if a bond salesman has been working for weeks to develop an attractive business opportunity with a client, he often does not inform his investment banking counterpart of the prospect for fear of having to split the revenue evenly, although the investment banker may be able to assist in closing the deal through connections at the company. Meanwhile, the client receives disjointed and incomplete service despite our claim to be a "full-service" investment bank.

My solution is simple, although administratively more time-consuming. Allocate 100 percent of the revenue to each division involved, and at the year-end compensation review delve past the quantity of the revenue to determine the quality of the individual's contribution. For product development, allocate expenses to a general corporate account if the product is deemed worthy. Such a qualitative system for internal accounting imposes the burden of considering individual cases. However, within an industry bred on innovative products and integrated services, stagnation due to internal competition will result in long-term detrimental effects.

My Harvard experience was shaped by my work at Phillips Brooks House (PBH), Harvard's volunteer community service/action coordinating center (see resume). The community exposure that PBH afforded me brought to life the material in my courses. PBH provided me with a sense of purpose and the opportunity to help, both of which I felt a need to fulfill. While at PBH I realized that I enjoyed running a large organization and that my strengths lay in working with and organizing people.

After college I received a Rockefeller Fellowship which allowed me to spend nine months traveling through Asia, followed by six months of development work in Sri Lanka (see resume). Throughout my travels I was fascinated by the economic and social development of the societies I visited. In particular I found my attention was drawn to organizations either spurring, or being driven by, this development.

My observations kept returning to one common thread: no matter how original the concept, no matter how good the plan, no matter how plentiful the resources, the success of an organization was dependent upon how well it was run. What looked good on paper so often fell short due to lack of control, leadership, or efficiency. Conversely, organizations that were managed effectively often achieved what seemed impossible on paper.

My work in Sri Lanka further crystallized this point. I lived in a small village in the Hill Country where I participated in the writing of a proposal aimed at generating jobs and income for this deprived region. My research and observations made clear the desperate dearth of managers. Coops, cottage industries, development projects, loan funds, and government programs were crippled by inefficiency, disorganization, and bureaucracy. Sisira Nawaratne, the man with whom I wrote the proposal, has dedicated his life to addressing this problem and, in so doing, has provided a role model for me. His ability to turn these organizations around demonstrated that a creative manager has the potential to make the contributions to others that I hope to make during my lifetime.

The last part of my stay in Sri Lanka provided me with a very disturbing example of the importance of good management. A terrible life shattering riot broke out between the Sinhalese and the Tamils, the two main ethnic groups in the country. The Tamils were maimed, tortured, burned out. What lives they had left could only continue within the confines of a refugee camp. Fifteen camps had sprung up for the 90,000 homeless Tamils in the country's capital city, Colombo. Development workers were asked by the government to help run the camps. I volunteered along with four friends to run one of the camps, a small missionary school for 500 day students, now inundated with 4,000 homeless refugees.

The memory of my first sight of the camp will haunt me forever. People were everywhere, huddled in groups, some silently sobbing, some shrieking out their agony, others just staring off into space contemplating the void their lives had become. The temperature hovered close to 100 degrees. Many of the refugees had not eaten or bathed for two days and were coated with the dust in which they had been sleeping. There were long lines and fights for the very limited food and two working water spigots. Flies were everywhere. The whole area was walled in and guards stood nervously outside keeping watch for the mobs that roamed the city.

After organizing the camp structurally, we tried to meet the basic physical and emotional needs of its population. Over the next five days I found myself being psychologist, chef, nurse, plumber, arbitrator, entertainer, and all too often, dictator. One moment I was unclogging a toilet with my hands, the next trying to explain to someone why his life, as he had known it, had just ended. I felt elation as we created the camp's first shower by running a hose from a neighbor's house, followed by fear as we called in the guards to break up a food fight.

During my time in the camp I gained a tremendous insight into myself. I am as proud of my contributions during that time as I am of anything I have ever done. Working together to turn that camp from a nightmare into a functioning, albeit sad and woefully inadequate, environment was the most challenging endeavor in which I have been involved. The satisfaction I derived from my contributions to that effort helped to ease the horror of the situation. Even under those circumstances I found fulfillment in organizing chaos and making things work.

When I returned to the United States I took a job campaigning for [a Senator] in his United States Senate race. I ended up running the campaign headquarters, managing the full-time volunteers, setting up the computer operation and coordinating the election day activities. These tasks offered me the chance to use my creativity, leadership skills and organizational ability. I enjoyed working closely with a large group of people to achieve a finite goal with a strict deadline and limited resources.

The campaign was my first real introduction to politics. While I learned a lot about electoral politics, I realized I wanted to learn more broadly about government. A CORO Fellowship seemed the best way to do that. A CORO Fellowship is a nine month leadership training program in which twelve people rotate through a series of internships in government, business, labor, community and political organizations (see resume). As I moved through the internships I saw the connections, interdependence, and complexity of these organizations. I learned how almost any decision made by those in charge is influenced by the interaction between sectors. I not only became aware of the importance of good managers, I realized that many of the skills that made for a good manager in the public sector were the same as the skills vital to success in the private sector. Over and over again we interviewed leaders who had moved between jobs in business, government, politics, and non-profits. Consistently, they stressed the commonality of skills required to be successful in various fields.

My current job as [an assistant in Mayor Koch's administration] has given me the best exposure imaginable to the consequences of good and bad management. One of our main responsibilities is to be the Mayor's eyes and ears at the Metropolitan Transportation Authority (MTA). This Authority, which has the responsibility for running the world's largest transportation system, suffers from a legacy of mismanagement which includes misallocation of resources, improper accounting, and indefinitely deferred maintenance. Supervision and accountability were lacking or non-existent. Its history provides a textbook example of how not to run an organization.

The managers currently running the MTA are charged with trying to reverse this history of neglect as quickly as possible, using severely limited resources. The management reforms they have introduced and their triage approach to efficiently stabilizing the system, are slowly starting to show dividends. A political environment, however, demands quick results. Watching these officials attempting to run the MTA like a business, while at the same time balancing political pressures, has been a tremendous learning experience.

This job also has shown me how much more I need to learn about the technical skills of management before I will be prepared to help effectively run a large organization. This is the appropriate time to seek out that training, and I am convinced that [your school], for the reasons outlined in the following essay, is the best school for me.

I assumed my most challenging leadership role during the two and one-half years that I was [a major newspaper's] bureau chief and correspondent in Mexico City. I arrived in 1983, at a time when Mexico's foreign debt crisis supposedly was solved. But I soon learned otherwise by probing behind the veil of official secrecy and rhetoric.

Because of the importance of Mexico to my newspaper's readership, I felt it was my responsibility to examine the growing economic and political pressures quietly building within the unique Mexican system. I canvassed leading industrialists, politicians, diplomats and labor leaders to obtain clues to political and economic trends. To stay abreast of social developments, I interviewed housewives, urban slum dwellers, social activists and rural peasants. I produced revealing stories on the Mexican political system, on various industries and financial markets, and on the contest of wills between the embattled private sector and the government. As a result, I was able to show long before my competitors how Mexico was derailing its own economic recovery plans.

In 1985, [my paper] assigned a special team of reporters and editors to produce a major series of page-one articles on Mexico; I provided sources, information and support to the entire team. I also co-wrote the opening and closing articles of the series. Mexico City was struck by the devastating earthquake of 1985 before we could complete our project. Under extremely difficult circumstances, I was able to refocus our efforts and report additional material to show how the government's mismanagement of the crisis had worsened its political problems. The Mexico series was among the coverage that won [the paper] a major prize for international reporting in 1986.

Throughout most of this period, I was the newspaper's sole representative in Mexico, making me a public figure in a country vitally concerned with its international image as portrayed by foreign correspondents. The government continually tried to exert pressure on foreign reporters to change their coverage; when I refused to bend to their pressures I was singled out as a favorite target for government-inspired attacks in the Mexican press. Yet, I managed to deal with this criticism in a way that enhanced my newpaper's reputation in Mexico and actually increased our access to influential news sources.

In the U.S., I've often assumed leadership responsibilities beyond my specific job duties. I have helped manage news bureaus on several occasions during extended absences of my supervisors. I've often helped guide younger or more inexperienced reporters and coordinated news coverage with other news bureaus when unexpected news developments arose. I also have wide experience responding to comments and complaints about our published articles. I've also served as a spokesman for [the paper] in appearances before community and business groups. On many occasions, I've been able to draw on the management experiences I had during college, when I was editor-in-chief of a full-sized daily newspaper written and edited by student journalists.

Both abroad and in the U.S. I believe I have demonstrated managerial potential through my ability to work with and motivate many different types of people. I've been able to sort out my own work priorities and guide the work of others in order to produce high-quality work under intense time pressure. And I've earned a reputation among my peers for my analytical abilities, writing skills, and solid dependability.

Essays About the MBA

This should be the easiest essay to write. You've probably gone through all the arguments for and against business school a hundred times while deciding whether to go. Now all you have to do is put your thoughts on paper clearly and coherently.

You should use this type of essay to convince admission officers—as you have already convinced yourself—that you could advance so much farther in your career and contribute so much more to society if you had an MBA. If you can provide examples of previous accomplishments and show that you *need* more business education for continued success, your application will be hard to ignore.

Many of the applicants in this group had reached an impasse in their careers. Many opted for business school to learn the skills needed to tackle more innovative projects. Others, especially reporters and advertising people, saw a need in their industry to bridge the gap between the creative people and the "front office." They knew that adding business knowledge to their creative talents could make them proficient executives who would also understand their less financially-minded employees.

Other applicants felt that their lack of an MBA was limiting their future options and pushing them onto unfulfilling career tracks. They wanted to acquire business skills that could combine with their present talents to open up more rewarding opportunities.

However, explaining how an MBA would help you is the easy part. After all, most people would be better off with an MBA. Your task is to analyze your goals carefully and demonstrate why you should be one of the privileged few who receives top business training. Why would *you* be more valuable to society with an MBA than the other 5,000 applicants?

Simply put, if you can convince an admissions officer that you *will* be more valuable with an MBA than the others, your essay will be successful.

There is an old Chinese saying: "The value of a sword cannot be judged when the sword stands alone in a corner; only when it is wielded by an expert can one see its true worth." That is how I think of an MBA.

I have worked with quite a few account executives who have MBAs and I find them, as a rule, more competent and rounded than their non-MBA counterparts. There are certain things that are intrinsic to possesors of graduate degrees; they are slightly older, they are intelligent enough to be accepted into degree programs, they have learned (one way or another) to deal with the work required to earn their degrees, and they've had to work closely with people not of their choosing. So in a way, MBAs are broken-in. They're used to inordinate amounts of work with people they may not necessarily like or respect, frightening deadlines and thinking so hard they almost bleed from their ears. They've been through "Basic".

However, the AEs I've worked with got hired at some pretty incredible salaries and I'm not sure all of them were worth it. Some, yes. All, no. I think the main problem was a large percentage of them had 4 years of undergrad, then 3 years of B-School *before* their first job. No Real-World experience, no Real-World judgement. And that was their Achillies' heel. They were well-versed in theory, but hell, in theory, a bumble bee can't fly.

I think many of the problems they caused could have been avoided if all MBA programs required 4 or 5 years of work experience. See how far *that* idea gets with this "gotta-be-a-millionaire-by-the-time-I'm-thirty" generation. A lot of them

figure an MBA is the ticket to The Good Life. Very possibly.
Corporations wine and dine B-Schoolers in their Junior year,
for crissakes. Hell, I knew a Harvard kid who was a star, and
these multi-nationals were falling all over each other to get on
his dance card. He scored a summer internship in a finance
company that paid him more for a summer than I made last
year, and I ain't doing bad. They guaranteed him a job after he
graduated. Eighty-five G's. Go figure. And I still can't decide if
the MBA made him worth that much or if he was a natural-
born finance-Einstein.

Some guys take an MBA, get into a little company and make
it sing. Bango. "New Faces" in Forbes. Others, well, there's the
story of Harley-Davidson. It was acquired by AMF. They sent
in a team of hot-shot MBAs. An MBA's job is to make money.
Make a profit, then increase profits. I figure they were "Punk"
MBAs (like the ones I mentioned before. . . first job right out of
school, very mercenary). They probably figured that if they
turned enough of a profit, AMF would promote them out of
there or they would use their successes to jump to another
company *before* the long-term effects of their decisions became
evident. I can't testify to that; all I know is that the quality of
the company's products went straight down the flusher and in
three years, you couldn't give those things away. Bikers were
turning to Hondas. Harleys could belch up their insides at any
moment. Cheap materials and cheaper techniques. Non-existent
quality control. And the new models went totally against the
grain of the true Harley buyer. They even tried to market a
cafe racer, which was as European as Brie, to a buyer who
would only eat Apple Pie. It was total disregard for their
primary market and total delusion to think they could turn a
Hog into a Thoroughbred and that anyone would buy such an
odd creature as other than a curiosity. I *can* testify to those
results. I worked in a motorcycle shop then.

Anyway, AMF didn't put up a fight when Harley wanted to
go independant. Everyone blamed the Bean Counters for the
screw-ups. The Managers. Bottom-Liners. They short-termed
the company to the brink of extinction.

The strengths and weaknesses of an MBA? Look not to the
sword, but to the swordsman.

I want to shepherd Earth's move into Space. That is, I want to be one of the people responsible for removing the barriers preventing the productive use and exploration of Space. The knowledge and experience I have gained at Cornell, Citibank, and NASA's Johnson Space Center will help me accomplish this task. The two career goals I discuss here result from my analysis of the risks endangering the movement I want to encourage.

Many of the technical risks involved in going to and living in Space for long periods of time have been solved. For example, the American, European, Canadian, and Japanese Space Station will have a closed water system. This recycling of water will make room for other supplies on the logistics flights serving the Space Station. Solutions like the closed water systems are expensive. The aerospace industry is working hard to lower these costs.

Those technical risks that still exist do not trouble me. I have found many people at Cornell and NASA excited about producing the engineering refinements needed to make the technical risks of space travel and exploration negligible. I want to provide them the opportunities to make those advances by reducing the financial, political, and organizational risks associated with the development of space.

The prime financial risks associated with investment in Space result not the failure of one or two projects, but from investors' inability to recognize when good investments can be made in space systems. Strategies to remedy the financial sector's inability to evaluate investments in space systems call for a gradual approach so investors can learn how to profit from space ventures. In the case of private launch systems, this gradual approach requires some project such as the development of a simple, small scale launch system. My work at Citibank and in political economy courses at Cornell has convinced me that this system must serve a realistic need. Several companies, including Space Services Inc. of Houston have tried unsuccessfully to market simple launch vehicles. These companies have produced launch systems without aiming their product at any particular set of customers. In an earth-bound analogy, they are providing only a truck when they must first find a customer who needs some sort of transportation.

The need to provide a service to a customer in space leads to one conclusion. For the foreseeable future, the one and only customer is the International Space Station. Research at the Johnson Space Center indicates that the logistics needs of the Space Station cannot be met by the Space Shuttle alone. Under this condition, the most likely venture to fulfill a need of this customer is one that can ensure the accurate and speedy delivery of small payloads to the Space Station. I plan to create an organization to provide this service within the first few years after I complete business school. Such a venture would require a moderate amount of capital. The key technology, safe operations in proximity to the Space Station, would be transferable to other ventures such as satellite refueling. The lessons learned in this undertaking would reduce the uncertainties for subsequent payload systems development and thus reduce the associated financial risks.

Success in a project like this would have the same beneficial effects on general space haulage that the U.S. Postal Service's early use of airmail had on the aviation industry. In conjunction with decreased costs resulting from new technology and program experience, the success of the small payload service would make other commercial systems possible. The increased availability of spares parts on the Space Station provided by this service would reduce the risks associated with designing and operating commercial payloads on the station.

The small payload service can only serve as part of a larger strategy to reduce the risks of going to Space. Additional actions must be taken to overcome the economic, institutional, and political risks of building an infrastructure where no industry exists and of manufacturing a product where no infrastructure exists. Work I did for several government courses I took at Cornell convinced me that societies manage risk by creating institutions. In a closely related example, NASA was born out of the National Advisory Committee for Aeronautics as part of the reaction to the risks posed by Sputnik. My plans are based upon expectations that a similar type of behavior will be repeated in dealing with the problem of space commercialization. To be specific, I want to be responsible for the division of NASA as it exists now into a research and exploration agency and a space infrastructure agency. NASA needs to be split up because its research goals conflict with its operational goals. This conflict manifests itself in many ways. Currently, flight equipment is designed so that it has many potential uses. This suits the research side of NASA. Operations philosophy, on the other hand, calls for simple dedicated equipment that fills only a limited set of operational requirements. Simplicity and limited scope make operational equipment reliable and inexpensive.

The research and exploration agency would draw upon the parts of NASA responsible for successes like the Apollo and the Voyager programs. The infrastructure agency would have its roots in NASA's current Space Shuttle and Space Station programs. Such an operations agency would eventually be made a private company or dissolved in favor of private organizations. Talk of this division has already surfaced as a result of the Challenger accident. Dr. Fletcher, NASA's Administrator, has recently announced a reorganization of NASA designed to forestall this breakup. With the eventual split, each agency will have a distinct role and also a distinct set of problems. I want to take on the challenge of minimizing those problems by being the one responsible for the transition of NASA into those two new agencies.

The role of the research and exploration agency will be much the same as the role the space research sections of NASA had up through the Soviet-American Apollo-Soyez Test Project in 1975. Its role will also encompass the aeronautical investigations that NASA does. I recognize the possibility that this agency can easily be forgotten if it does not run programs such as a Manned Mars Mission that capture the public's imagination. Still, this possibility is not a valid argument against splitting up NASA. The level of funding for space research should be a legislative decision. If the public is persuaded that this agency is necessary, it will get the funds it needs.

To make this agency work, its organization must promote the development of clear research and exploration goals without stifling creativity and discovery. This requires excellent communications within the agency. The leaders of the research and engineering organization will need to change the way NASA manages its research organization now if they want to improve communications. I expect to learn how to manage that change while at the School of Management.

As one of the creators of the space infrastructure agency, I must find a way to build the infrastructure necessary for industry in Space to be viable. To do this, the space infrastructure agency must fulfill the role of the market in both the launch vehicle and space industry sectors. Foremost, the agency must provide the incentives and information that markets in more mature sectors generate. Comsat, in creating a domestic and international market for U.S. satellite manufacturers has performed this role for the communications satellite industry. I understand that to recreate Comsat's success in a different sector, under different external economic conditions will require skill, hard work, and luck. Here again, the School of Management can provide the skills I need.

I have described lofty goals here in more ways than one. I have chosen these goals because they motivate me and because I know that even if I do not attain them completely, I will still be satisfied. To get close to achieving these goals, I need to become better at making risky decisions and recovering from poor ones. My work at Cornell, Citibank, and NASA has brought me to the point where I can identify the risks I must overcome to achieve the goals I have chosen. The knowledge and confidence I gain at business school will allow me to run a small package delivery service to orbit successfully. That experience, in turn, will prepare me to manage the creation of the two new agencies out of NASA that I see as necessary to promote Earth's move into Space.

The pattern of my life, the series of choices I have made, has been shaped by two divergent tendencies: a tendency toward idealism and a tendency toward pragmatism. At extremes, I have made clay bricks to build a primary school in rural Africa, and I have worked in the largest law firm in Boston. At times I have been frustrated by the seeming incompatibility of these two tendencies, and yet I value them both. Fortunately, I have discovered that my idealism and my pragmatism converge in a way that I find deeply satisfying in the field of arts management.

In stating that my career goal is to be an arts manager, I invite three questions: Why management? Why art? And why the two together?

Why Management? I believe that I possess certain strengths and qualities which are essential for a good manager, notably: social skills, organizational ability, resourcefulness, analytical ability, and a fund of knowledge. In both my education and my work experience I have made choices which have allowed me to utilize and develop these strengths and qualities. My desire to be a professional manager stems from the satisfaction I get from using them.

I like people, and I have developed the skills needed to work with a wide variety of personalities. In 1982, when I worked at a bluegrass music festival as Assistant to the Producer, I interacted with everyone from the county fire chief to the owners of a vegetarian food stand, from dozens of eager volunteer staff members to an audience member who complained about the

size and shape of his neighbor's lawn chair, and from newspaper reporters to the lead musicians—literally hundreds of
people during the four days of the festival. In my current position as Director of Development at an Off-Broadway style
theatre I work closely with the Board of Directors. The twenty-
three directors present a variety of personalities, backgrounds
and expectations that I must accomodate, while trying to ad-
vocate my own views, in our frequent meetings. These two experiences have added breadth and depth, respectively, to my
social skills.

Perhaps my greatest strength is my ability to organize. Most
recently, I have used this skill in producing fundraising events.
The first step of course is to design an event that will appeal to
potential donors and thus generate maximum income. The
organizational challenge is then to solve a myriad of logistical
problems including invitations, decorations, music, food and
drink. I must make sure that each task is assigned to a
volunteer on the events committee and that the volunteers
complete their jobs on time. Ultimately I serve as the coordinator of the parts, the manager of the details.

My current job also demands that I be very resourceful. The
Theatre Project Company has only nine full-time staff members
to run a professional mainstage theatre and a touring children's
theatre company. As a result, each staff member has a tremendous amount of responsibility and often has to wear more than
one hat. Furthermore, the Theatre's chronic lack of financial
resources creates numerous problems for which the staff must
find quick and creative solutions. Last summer, due to an un-
fortunate set of circumstances, the Theatre found itself without
a Business Manager. I took on this position, in addition to
holding my own position, for two and a half months until a
new Business Manager was hired. When I started, I knew
nothing about accounting or financial management, but among
other tasks I had to keep the Company's books, file the final
financial report for our season with the state arts council, handle all disbursements and receivables, and do the weekly
payroll. For the most part, I learned by doing. It was at once
exhausting and exhilerating.

My undergraduate education at Yale helped me develop my
analytical ability. As an English major, I wrote many essays.

In each case I had to examine a piece of literature, extract the important bits of information (i.e. the information relevant to my essay topic), and then organize those bits of information into a coherent statement. This was particularly difficult in the case of my senior thesis. I chose to write about the work of South African playwright Athol Fugard, and at the time there were no secondary sources to aid me in my analysis. I was a critical pioneer: I read all of his plays, probing each one deeply, and tried to determine the essence of his work. Undoubtedly, the essay on Fugard represents some of the finest work I did while at Yale. I continue to use my analytical ability, the ability to separate a whole into its constituents for examination and interpretation, in less formal, less academic ways. For example, whenever I write a corporate or foundation grant proposal for the Theatre, I review the potential donor's application guidelines, determine which of our programs fall within those guidelines, and decide which aspects of the Theatre's history and activities need emphasis in the proposal.

Thus far I have limited my discussion of managerial strengths and qualities to skills. While not a skill, a fund of knowledge is essential for a good manager. By "fund of knowledge" I mean a large body of specific information, gleaned from formal education and from experience. The acquisition of knowledge always has been one of my goals. Philosophically I agree with the goals of a liberal arts education, and at Yale I took a wide variety of courses. Outside of my education also I have sought to expose myself to numerous situations and ideas, through travel, athletics and voluntarism.

Why art? It is difficult to talk about art without sounding either silly or sententious, even if sincere. I believe, however, that it is the responsibility of professionals in the arts to articulate the value of art to society.

Through their work artists offer the other members of society a new perspective, a chance to stand in someone else's shoes, even if only for a short while. In accepting their offer, we acquire knowledge, knowledge which may help us to better ourselves and our world. Art enlightens.

Furthermore, art has the rare power to create community. Art is produced for people to see or hear; it is meant to be shared. In an age when both the church and the family are disintegrating, art can still bring people and their ideas together. Art transcends differences among individuals.

For as long as I can remember I have believed that art is important. The knowledge I have gained from my literature studies at Yale, my jobs in the arts, and my participation in various cultural activities has enhanced my innate appreciation of art.

Why the two together? Management is what I'm good at; art is what I believe in. Together they provide an intellectual and emotional balance which I find personally satisfying. More importantly, I am convinced that this balance will enable me to work to my fullest and thus make the greatest possible contribution to society.

The question: "What professional goals have you tentatively established for the next five years of your life and how do you see the MBA helping you reach your goals?"

Funny you should ask. I'm right in the middle of a five-year plan right now. My original plan involved leaving New York and working my way west. New York City *is* Madison Avenue, but the compromises necessary to live there were simply too great. I planned to stay in Detroit two years, move on to Chicago for three or four years, then San Francisco, then Boston. If I fell in love with a location or job along the way, maybe I'd settle down. I haven't found what I'm looking for in Detroit. I got stalled here, but fortunately, this stall has allowed me a rare glimpse at the upper echelons of an advertising agency.

I noticed that the majority of the people upstairs weren't advertising people. That is, the ability to do fabulous advertising or even to recognize it was not a prerequisite. Rather, they were business men. Unfortunately, they were *merely* business men. If they had been great advertising men, they could have been so much more. And so could our company. It was then that I realized what I could do if I combined my abilities and talents in Advertising with what it took to be a "business man". Hence the first thoughts of B-School.

You see, as a "Creative" in an advertising agency, I can become a Creative Director or, at most, Executive Creative Director. Not good enough. I needed more options. (It is my adamant belief that a good life is the result of many options chosen well.)

When I worked at The Big J. Walter in N.Y., I had occasion to participate in several New Business Pitches. They were wonderous things. Up all night, doing six or seven campaigns on as many marketing strategies. Adrenaline flowing, living on coffee and cigarettes. Packing it all up and going to the Presentation like hitting a beach-head. It was the guerrilla warfare of Advertising. ("I love the smell of markers in the morning. It smells like. . . New Business!") And I miss it terribly. People tell me it's very much like the so-called "Viet Nam Syndrome". I believe them.

Anyway, I'd like to get to Chicago in the next few years, preferably heading up a New Business team. I'm torn between wanting to work for a huge agency or a tiny one. A large agency would offer me unlimited resources, multi-faceted personell, higher (and more expensive) technology, and all the dogs and ponies you need to bowl over a prospective client. But a smaller agency has a lot going for it, too. By the size alone, there is a lack of weight and inertia. When you decide to do something, you *do* it. (Try that in J. Walter.) It allows you to be fleet of foot, quick to react, quick to change. Built for speed and handling, as they say in The Motor City. Also, by picking a small shop with great potential, I could get in the ground floor. Then I could be one of the people who *make* it famous.

I'm hoping with an MBA in Marketing (the skills are more important to me than the degree), I'll get a few offers from Chicago agencies to do just those things. Then, by landing accounts, I'd set up my own group, as a Creative Director. And with the MBA, I'd be able to think like a Suit (our term for Account Executives). Think of the possibilities! I'd be a sort of Jekyl/Hyde fellow, or a Frankenstein creation, with the brain of a marketing-oriented Account Executive and the soul of a wild, crazy, free-thinking Creative. A frightening picture, what?

The main thing an MBA would do is give me options. Right now, I'm starting to run out of them. It's kind of a nice situation to be in. . . running out of options is one of the prices of achieving the goals you've set for yourself. With an MBA *plus* my advertising background, I could be very valuable to a company like P&G (Proctor and God). Or I could go into consulting. Or, yes, I could start my own shop. As I said, I like to have options. Lots of them. And an MBA would be, as they say, just the ticket.

Essays About Accomplishments

Some of the accomplishments in this group of essays are extraordinary. One applicant helped raise $2 million through a direct-mail campaign, while another founded a novel, non-profit corporation that was praised by the national media. A third person started a small airline—while he was still in college!

Most likely, you haven't done anything quite so spectacular, but don't let that discourage you. If you're not sure which of your accomplishments you're most proud of, read through this chapter with an eye for the similarities among these applicants. Each one was confronted with a difficult problem and solved it with creativity. They were confident and innovative enough to improvise when unique situations arose. And they succeeded. It's that quality—the bold, entrepreneurial spirit—that many admissions officers told us they admire.

So when you're choosing your finest accomplishment, try to look for an instance when you solved a tough problem with an unconventional insight, or took an entrepreneurial path around the bureaucracy to get something done.

Remember, the actual accomplishment is often not important. What admissions officers want to see is how you *think* about a task—and how effectively you can communicate your thoughts in an essay.

I began my career as a scientist, but I am now director of a corporation I founded and developed. In 1982 I began planning a national gene bank of the rarest American plant types. *Time* called the organization I started and now direct "an unprecedented program, by far the most comprehensive to date." *Science*, *The New York Times*, *Washington Post*, and Associated Press network, among others, have all featured major stories about it.

I have learned that I can set ambitious goals for an organization, attract financial support, build an effective staff, and most importantly, produce results. It is far more satisfying than the technical work I did previously, and convinces me that my career will continue in business administration. At the same time, I do not consider myself an excellent manager; I often improvise when I should be able to rely on practiced skills and an informed sense of perspective. I need formal training to sharpen the entrepreneurial and managerial skills I have developed.

I particularly want to attend your school because of its unsurpassed reputation for training general business managers able to function in environments that demand scientific and quantitative abilities. The integration of business training with my knowledge of the basic sciences would give me powerful skills for work in the high technology industries. Biotechnology, in particular, is only now becoming a true economic activity. I am convinced that there are many unrealized opportunities to develop simple, extremely useful applications of existing biotechnologies, such as screening plants used in non-western medicine for active pharmaceuticals. No U.S. drug company is now investigating such plants, although a quarter of all present prescription medicines are plant derivatives. Nonetheless, I view my past training as a possible asset to my career, not a constraint; I would expect study at your school to broaden my perspective on possible careers, as well as providing substantive information.

My commitment to a career in management has developed slowly. When I was an undergraduate, I was the student founder and resident director of Shaw House, the "residential college" for the Boston College Honor's program. I organized a program intended to be an intellectual and cultural focus for the House, the Program as a whole, and the entire residential campus. Later, while I was in graduate school, I was one of two leaders of research expeditions with about twenty participants. These trips have taken me to uninhabited islands and coastal jungles in the Caribbean, Central America and Africa. Leading the expeditions demonstrated to me that I could build an effective, task-oriented group. But at the time, I saw both of these activities as secondary to my studies in basic biology and resource management.

Within a few years after graduate school, I began planning the Center for Plant Conservation, now the national gene bank for rare American plant types. I designed the Center as a nonprofit corporation, but one focussed on measurable accomplishment. It is rapidly building a permanent genetic reserve of over 3,000 plant types, almost all of which were previously inaccessible and likely to be lost entirely.

The Center combines twenty-five of the most notable scientific institutions in the United States—including Harvard, the Smithsonian and the Department of Agriculture—in a program well beyond the capacity of any preexisting organization. While the Center was the first program of its kind, several countries, including mainland China, are considering it as a model for plant genetic reserves of their own. The Canadian Centre for Plant Conservation is already operating.

I conceived of the Center five years ago. Today it is a major not-for-profit corporation with a structure analogous to a commercial franchising chain. More than sixty scientists and technicians at institutions throughout the country are building collections of living plants, seeds and tissue cultures as part of the Center's program, and a staff of seven, including three with Ph.D.s, a J.D. and an M.B.A., coordinates its operations at the national level.

Building the Center has refined all my basic abilities, strengthening some and tempering others. More than any other experience, it has helped me develop both the external abilities and internal qualities of leadership—and there is little of my experience that is not required of me as a leader of a rapidly growing organization.

While I was still in school I saw my organizational roles as secondary to my scientific training. I am now convinced that my technical education is background for a career in management.

Gaining employment as a management consultant with [a prestigious consulting firm] is my most significant accomplishment to date. I value this achievement for it demonstrates my ability to create and take advantage of opportunity. As a general rule, [the firm] is extremely selective in hiring consultants. Interested candidates must possess intellectual ability, communication skills, maturity, and potential for career advancement. Minimum credentials for employment generally include an advanced degree from a first-rate program and/or an industry specialty gained only through five to ten years of intense work experience. As a consultant in the San Francisco practice, I am the youngest of thirty-one consultants and only one of six without a graduate degree. Moreover, prior to joining the consulting staff, I had only fifteen months of full-time work experience.

My second most significant accomplishment is receiving an offer to perform with the Continental Company of Ice Capades. Prior to enrolling at Berkeley, I seriously considered a career in professional figure skating. For five years, my weekly schedule included fourteen hours of ice time practice and three hours of individualized instruction from a certified professional. I skated competitively for two years and performed in numerous amateur exhibitions. On February 18, 1981, I auditioned for and received an offer to skate in a line position with Ice Capades. After a month of deliberation, I declined the skating offer; my desire for a university education and a career in management significantly outweighed the possibility of a short-lived skating career. I value my skating achievement as it demonstrates my motivation, self-discipline, determination, and capacity to sustain an extraordinary high level of physical and mental energy.

My involvement with Collegiate Air Service as President and Founder and my work overseeing the leasing program for Biltmore Place in downtown Los Angeles both illustrate my project management and leadership abilities. While my positions with Collegiate Air Service and with Biltmore Place were very different, both required an able project manager and leadership in order to succeed. In each instance, I managed the process of bringing human and capital resources together to fulfill a need. My involvement was instrumental in realizing certain objectives and in maximizing value.

While my activity with the flying service occurred more than three years ago, it is a significant achievement that illustrates my entrepreneurial and managerial skills from an early age. Early in my senior year of college, I was frustrated with my difficulty in building the airtime required for advanced pilot ratings. The cost of flying a two-seat, single-engine plane was prohibitive, not to mention the significantly larger cost of twin-engine aircraft. My objective was to log flight time at a relatively low cost in as large and complex an aircraft as possible. My idea was to provide the University community with an airtaxi service. This would fulfill my objectives and provide customers with a low-cost means of transportation. I consulted an aviation attorney, insurance agents, and a local fixed base operator (a plane leasing company) to determine the feasibility of setting up such a service. At first, there were questions regarding compliance with FAA regulations, liability, and licensing which were all quickly solved. I set up the service as a nonprofit organization to avoid the arduous and expensive licensing process. Overhead for the venture was extremely low because my only expenses were the attorney's fees, insurance costs, and limited marketing materials explaining the service. A fleet of planes with four to nine seats were put at my disposal. My only obligation to the fixed base operator was payment for the actual time the aircraft was used. I contacted other students who were qualified pilots and explained to them the idea and the opportunities it offered them. Three other pilots agreed to fly for the service. I instituted certain policies and procedures for running the operation which included performance standards, weather minimums, schedules for pilot availability, and billing procedures. It was a thrilling experience to create a small nonprofit airtaxi operation from what was originally an idea to maximize my airtime. During the year, we logged approximately 60 hours of flight time worth over $4,500.

A more recent example of my leadership abilities and managerial potential is my work as a member of the on-site development team overseeing the renovation and construction of the Biltmore Hotel and complex (Biltmore Place)—a mixed-use project comprised of 410,000 square feet of office space, 707 hotel rooms, 30,000 square feet of retail space, and a 368 stall above-ground garage. One of my major duties was to oversee the in-house leasing staff. Acting as the owner's representative, I organized and managed the on-site brokers and directed them in their search for prospective tenants. I cultivated a large network of contacts with leasing brokers, tenant representatives, and building owners which better enabled me to gauge market trends. Using the information synthesized from the marketplace, I was able to direct the leasing efforts and the strategy of the brokers and to manage the expectations of the project owner.

A remote beach on the Gulf of Aqaba in what is now the Egyptian Sinai is not the ideal place to be stranded for three days with no food and little water. Except for these necessities, however, we had it all in those three days: prowling Bedouins, a sandstorm, and temperatures over 120°. While I emerged from this ordeal unscathed physically, it left an indelible mark on me as a person.

My odyssey into the desert was one of many adventures I had in the summer of 1979 with my Swedish and Swiss friends from the Weizmann Institute of Science in Israel. Before that summer I was the typical Canadian boy, I had done a bit of travelling with my family, but my views of the world were still fairly parochial. What I experienced for the first time was that the greatest excitement of travel was not just learning about the country of Israel, but about the people and life in Israel. This summer was memorable because of the new cultures I learned about but also because from the context of these cultures I had the opportunity to look back at my life in Canada with a wonderful new perspective. In comparison with life in Israel, Canada was a pretty cushy place to live. The focus of Israeli life is survival; there is a respect for life and a motivation which is unlike anything I have known in Canada.

It was a thirst for more of these experiences which inspired me to wander from the well worn path to Canadian universities and choose to head off to Harvard a year later. Canada and the United States may be among the most similar countries in the world, but when you grow up in one and then move to the other, the differences are striking. While the differences between the two cultures are not extreme when compared to Israel, people do have different attitudes and values. The last six and a half years in the United States have taught me a lot about Canada. It has shown me where Canada's real virtues lie and taught me not to take these for granted. Just as importantly, however, it has given me the opportunity to objectively view weaknesses in the Canadian way of life.

Like my experiences both in the U.S. and Israel, time I have spent in Australia, Sweden and Germany has been not just seeing a new country, but living with the "natives" and learning about their cultures and their lives. Like other trips abroad, each of these journeys has had a profound effect on my thoughts and personality. Each country has its own set of values which determine the relative importance of various things in life.

All of these experiences have made me a more sensitive and open-minded person and given me a more diverse perspective with which to deal with life. I look around me each day and see a lot of people who are got up in a world in which it is easy to take life and yourself too seriously. The idea of this work ethic would induce an incredulous expression on an Australian's face. I am grateful for the opportunities I have had to spend time abroad and to look back on the society in which I live from a wholly new context. It has helped me to deal with the pace of life in New York and kept my priorities in order.

In addition to this series of experiences abroad, I feel a number of more specific activities both at Harvard and at work have also contributed significantly to my personality and my goals for the future.

Strangely enough, when I look back at my Harvard days 20 years from now, my most vivid memories will probably be from the sport of rowing. Rowing is the ultimate synthesis of both individual and team excellence. I have never before and never since been tested so hard as an individual, both mentally and physically, but at the same time I have never felt so strongly the bonds of a team. A Harvard Crew alumnus commented to me once that he thought the greatest thing about rowing was that it could never become professional. No one would ever row for money. The motivation must come from much deeper than that.

Winter training disciplines the individual by spending long months of practice breaking through the "pain threshold". Whether it is racing up and down flight after flight of stadium steps in a raging blizzard, or staring into the counter of the ergometer as you pull your guts out, rowing strips away any pretense an individual may have and bares the real self, in terms of both mental and physical ability, to the world.

Just as winter training focuses on the individual, the coming of spring means the formation of a team. Once a boat gets on the water, the physical and mental capacities an individual oarsman has developed over the course of the year are utterly worthless unless they are directed toward the higher goal of team accomplishment. In a race one is not pulling for oneself anymore, but for one's fellow oarsmen. It is almost paradoxical that the fastest boats are always ones in which individual contribution is invisible.

Four years of rowing developed me into a much stronger more motivated person. While two years in New York is enough to dissolve one's physical strength, the mental strength I developed in rowing will never be lost. I was always a persistent person, but rowing gives whole new meaning to the word persistence. It gives you confidence in your ability to do almost anything that you put your mind to. On the other hand, rowing imparts a very strong sense of humility. It taught me that individual accomplishment is only of value if it benefits others. Finally, it showed me how much more meaningful any activity could be if it were done in the context of a group or team.

Harvard, however, meant more than developing brawn; it greatly transformed the intellectual side of my character. Through high school and the first three years of college academics were, for me, pretty superficial; an instructor told me something and I rewrote it later on a test to show that I was listening. My thesis in senior year at Harvard changed this attitude. The topic I chose to investigate was the social reform issue in mid-Victorian London as seen through the life of Henry Mayhew and his writings published in the series *London Labour and the London Poor*. The department I was in, Social Studies, was originally established to encourage the study of problems in the social sciences from a multi-disciplinary perspective (ie. history, social theory, economics, and political science). With this philosophy in mind, I found once I started researching my thesis that there were no bound-aries, and that I had to deal with the question in more dimensions than I had ever before contemplated. How did the social and cultural background of Mayhew create tension in his fundamentally reformist social attitudes? How did the political forces of the day cause the virtual censorship of his work? These are two of the countless issues which arose during the course of my study. This thesis showed me how much more stimulating an intellectual problem could be when looked at from different perspectives, and changed for good my approach to any problem. I am now much more careful in making sure my thoughts result from an analysis of different perspectives, and when others present a solution I am much more critical.

The last two and a half years [on Wall Street] have brought all of these divergent experiences together and helped refine my career goals. Like many analysts, the excitement of working on Wall Street left its mark on me in the first couple of years. One can be so swept up in the lifestyle that it is hard to imagine spending one's life working at anything else. In the last year, however, my attitudes towards the business have changed. During this time I have been immersed in work on two very large project finance assignments which have caused many of the career ideas I have developed over the last five years to crystalize.

For six months in 1985 and 1986 I was one member of a three-person team which advised the State Treasury of Queensland, Australia on what their role should be in the $1 billion development of the natural gas resources in the State. The Government's objective was to develop this resource so that they could lure more industry into the State. The objective of the private sector producers, who owned the rights to develop the gas, was to try to extract as much subsidy as possible from the State. As originally contemplated, our task was to advise the Government objectively on how to determine what level of subsidy, if any, was required to make the project happen. In reality, we became the conduit through which negotiations between the State and the producers flowed.

Our role as intermediary was particularly fascinating because I confronted, for the first time, the powerful influence politics can have on business. We could spend years developing the optimal approach, but political reality would always win the day.

84

It was only fitting that the Premier, Sir Joh Bjelke-Petersen, would choose the day when negotiating leverage for the Government was most crucial to announce in parliament that the Government would build the pipeline regardless of the required subsidy.

The second assignment was the project financing of a cogeneration facility to be built and operated by the private sector on the premises of the U.S. Army base at Fort Drum, New York. In developing the project from the ground up, I helped negotiate the contracts for construction, for fuel supply, and for the ultimate purchase of steam by the Army and electricity by Niagara Mohawk. In addition, I became involved with the engineers in learning about the circulating fluidized bed technology and was exposed to the negotiation of a labor contract with a union. In short, I was helping to build a standalone small business. As time went on I came to realize that while the financing was certainly important, all the other little pieces were just as important and often more interesting.

The business of an investment banker is, for the most part, one-dimensional; it is finance. Finance is certainly a very interesting subject and has been great fun to work in for the last two and a half years. While working on the Queensland and Fort Drum projects, however, I have become acquainted with other colors in the spectrum of business problems. Establishing career goals means thinking about the kind of things you would like to spend one-third of the rest of your life doing. The things I have learned at work have supplemented the attitude my thesis instilled and shown me the importance of having a job in which problems are multi-dimensional. To spend the rest of my life in the narrow world of finance is a little frightening regardless of the great experience I have had. With this realization I have set as my goal a career as a general manager in an industrial company rather than a specialized service company like an investment bank. From my experiences starting in high school, but most exemplified in rowing at Harvard and in the team environment at work, I have experienced the rewards which come from being the leader or manager of a group. I would hope to find a career where managing people and diverse business problems are the essence of the job.

Two years ago, I came to the Urban League of Eastern Massachusetts to volunteer my time to work in Boston's black community. As a social service organization, the Urban League is committed to seeing a better society. It provides a variety of different programs aimed at helping the community help itself. During my two years with the League, I have worked on and established several programs ranging from the Youth Leadership Program for neighborhood teenagers, to the Entrepreneur Incentive Committee aimed at encouraging minorities to become more involved in business, and to my current involvement as Committee Coordinator and mentor to adolescent fathers. My involvement in these programs has been sincere and committed to helping the community become a better place to live. I believe I offer the potential to develop into an active leader in the Boston business community. I want not only to establish a business here, but also to be responsible to the community in which I live and work. The Urban League has provided me with the opportunity to reach the community, and I believe that someday, I will provide opportunities for those same people who I am helping today.

I have a little book entitled "Things To Do This Life" and in it I list what I want to accomplish and when. Let me take you through some of the things under the "Career" heading.

I had chosen the field of advertising early in college, so naturally, Goal Number One was "Land a copywriting position in a major New York advertising agency." I landed a spot in probably the biggest agency in the world, as well as one of the best in marketing. Considering how competitive advertising has become in the last few years, I think this rates as my biggest and toughest achievement. Anyway, [the firm] had a myriad of accounts and plenty of opportunity. I stayed there almost four years, learning everything I could about advertising in general and copywriting in specific.

Then I diverged from my plans a bit. Goal Number Two was "Become the youngest Vice President ever appointed in the Creative Department." Instead, I got canned.

There's an old saying; "You're not really in advertising unless you've had a screaming match with your boss and lost." That problem could be looked upon as an opportunity in disguise, and it was, because it facilitated an easy transition into. . .

Goal Number Three: "Leave New York. Go to different cities and see what advertising is like around the country." The theory here is that once I've become a medium fish in a big pond, go to a small pond where I might be a Barracuda. So here I am in Michigan.

So a whole bunch of people here in Michigan already consider me a success. But what leads *me* to believe I'm a success? Well, most people in business say that you are *officially* a success in today's world if your salary is between one and one-and-one-half thousand dollars for every year of your age, and if I subscribed to the theory of money as a barometer of success, that would be a "Bingo". But there are lot of millionaires out there I wouldn't trust with a cat, and I *hate* cats. I believe there is a lot more to success than the number of digits after the dollar sign, and I think it is *that* attitude, *that* broadening of scope, that sets me up perfectly for the future.

Another reason I think I'm already a success is something else I'm involved in. For the past year, I have been the Executive Vice President of the Creative Advertising Club [in town]. (I'm President now.) We took a floundering professional organization that was losing members at an alarming rate, that was not performing any valuable service to the advertising community and that was the brunt of many a joke, and turned it completely around. The most recent CADDY Awards Show was one of the most successful in the 13 year history of the Club. As Executive Vice President, I had an awful lot to do with it.

All that makes me think I'll continue to succeed but like they say on late night TV, "Wait! There's more!" Yes, I manage to achieve most of the goals I set for myself, and yes, I've racked up an impressive list of credentials, and yes, I've got some real heavy-weights as recommenders. But my recommenders are bosses. Ask the kids, the young ones in the advertising community, what they think. Ask them if they think I'd make a good boss, or if they'd work for me. I'm not talking "leadership potential" here. I'm talking what I've *already* learned, what I can teach others *today* and what I've got to offer *now*. Yeah, it's great when the higher-ups give you the Good Housekeeping Seal of Approval, but it's nothing compared to what I feel when the phone rings and it's these kids calling for my advice and help. Now, *that's* success.

What I consider to be my third most substantial accomplishment is the most important because it is a perpetual feat. I grew up in a predominantly black neighborhood of Dorchester, Massachusetts, but I was educated until grade nine in a white school system in a suburb of Boston. I was told when I was in sixth grade, after taking a standardized test in which I was asked to discern the english meaning of certain mumbled words in a fictitious language, that I would be unsuccessful at learning a foreign language, and that it would be best not to enroll in a language course in junior high school. In the seventh grade I enrolled in French; needless to say, I have since become fluent. In my sophomore year of high school, I enrolled in Spanish, and through my continued studies at Harvard, I have acquired a thorough command of the Spanish language. This year I enrolled in elementary Portuguese with the intention to continue my studies individually, post-graduation, in order to achieve a level of fluency comparable to that which I have achieved in Spanish and French.

During high school, I was challenged, motivated and encouraged to become a genuine achiever. Nevertheless, I was discouraged from applying to Harvard, although I was President of the School, would graduate third in my class, and received superior SAT, Achievement and Advanced Placement scores.

I have never let the lack of economic resources which pervaded in my family discourage me from attaining my goals, for I viewed the financial aspect of my endeavors as a formality which I could overcome by seeking out scholarship assistance from various organizations and donors. I have become a role model for many individuals in my community and in my family. Yet many have questioned my ability to overcome my economic restraints and succeed. I frequently receive comments such as: "who would have ever thought that a girl from Dorchester would be at Harvard?" Through my achievements and as a role model, I hope to make that "phenomenon" less of a shock and more of a normality.

Extracurricular Essays

What do you do when you're not at work?

Who cares?

B-schools care, and with good reason. A lot of the best ideas come to a business person in the shower or at the bowling alley. Your work is part of an interrelated whole, and what you do out of the office has an impact on what you can do on the job. Consider how your behavior in your personal life affects or reflects your business life.

This type of essay also can make you likeable. The business world can be harsh, and you need to show what kind of humanity you can bring to it. A recent study in the *New York Times* reported that humor among office workers increases productivity and stimulates creative thought. Quirky, interesting, and humorous people make work and school more exciting. And they can certainly make an application essay more readable.

N•TROPY.

It's brief, candid, and it's what my license plate says. Entropy, the definition for the Second Law of Thermodynamics (Chemistry 012, spring 1982: see transcript), means "random disorder." Well, I'm not as random as I might like to think I am and I could never really be entirely disordered. Still, "spontaneous" wouldn't fit on one license plate.

I'm not limited in many ways; I've always done things simply because they excite me without considering the practicality involved, or not involved as the case may be. In high school, while the Boston Red Sox floundered and made ludicrous trades, I declared myself a "free agent fan" and notified every baseball team of my new status. I got some great responses . . . and a bunch of hats and T-shirts as a half-dozen teams competed for my services. I was very relieved when I finally received a letter from the Red Sox front office requesting that I reconsider my position; I did. Four years ago, when the Philadelphia Phillies were up for sale, I put in a bid to buy the team and was later notified by telegram that I had been outbid. Last semester came the crushing blow: ESPN notified me that I didn't meet *any* of the qualifications to be the Attorney they were looking for.

When it comes to the entertainment field I may be even more ambitious. During my freshman year, Duke was chosen as a site for some scenes in Douglas Trumball's *Brainstorm*. Though the set was closed to everyone not directly connected with the movie, I climbed through an unlocked basement window of the Duke Chapel and up to where the funeral (for

Louise Fletcher) scene was being shot. After spending the day making myself useful, when needed—lunchtime mostly, and invisible, when not, and getting to know many of the crew members, I was ecstatic when Mr. Trumball invited me back to help set up the next morning's wedding scene with Christopher Walken and Natalie Wood. The experience of those two days is as much an integral part of my education as any course I have taken.

Despite this adventurous, ambitious enthusiasm, I feel I am very responsible as the next essay will hopefully illustrate. I take my work very seriously but not to the point where I'm not aware of other people's feelings. I think my greatest ability is to make other people feel comfortable. My main interest is to generate a healthy working atmosphere and *then* a productive working atmosphere. I have the ability to be decisive yet open-minded, respectful yet productive, respected yet personable. My experiences at Duke have taught me a lot about working with people, something I enjoy doing very much.

Admittedly, some of my Duke experience *has* gone to my head but as long as I can realize this, then it's alright. Perhaps it's just that until I came to Duke I never had any true self-confidence. I had never really done anything for, and by, myself. Still, as I read over my application and essays, I'm astounded by the great number of "I" 's; I've always gotten greatest satisfaction out of sharing an experience. One of my favorite activitites is to play Santa Claus for local children and Duke students who can have their pictures taken with Santa. I have attached a photo—I'm the guy in the red. This year I broke the record I set last year by sitting for 528 pictures in five hours.

As for what areas I would like to develop more fully, one is certainly not my waistline (presently in the re-modeling stages). Though not really "fat", I have always been self-conscious about my appearance and I know that it has been the *one* thing that has always hindered my always feeling great about myself. Also, and I hope this doesn't hurt my chances for admission, my receding hairline has recently begun to "retreat." Not to push you or anything, but I'd like to think I'll have some hair to lose when I finally get to be a [management] student. Moreover, as a [management] student, I would be able to develop many skills which I have thus far been unable to perfect such as volleyball, surfing, and affection for PAC-10 basketball.

I think others perceive me very favorably. I smile a lot though probably laugh too much at my own jokes. A member of the President's Honor Council, I am also morally and ethically aware of the consequences of my actions as well as the actions themselves. Attempting to promote a sense of honor through vehicles such as symposiums, printed pamphlets, and public discussions is one of my greatest concerns this year. This does not mean that I would like to see an anti-personal honor code in effect but, rather, would like to make people comfortable following the dictates of their own conscience. Often, at a place like a University where the pressures to perform, get ahead, be accepted are so great, people sometimes forget what's really important and can be too willing to compromise their values to facilitate the realization of the objectives.

I've never been afraid to take risks because the consequences of not taking risks are too great and the benefits, unfulfilling. I sometimes think Duke took a great risk in accepting me four years ago. I believe my attending Duke has proven mutually beneficial. I would very much like to attend [your school]. I'm not really very familiar with [your city], or even California for that matter, but I think I could pick up and go and do just fine. After all, the Dodgers did it.

I was brought up in a family that was internationally oriented, and intellectually and culturally open and diverse. My father was Chairman of the Islamic Art Department at the Metropolitan Museum of Art in New York and a Professor at the Institute of Fine Arts of New York University. My mother is an archeologist specializing in Byzantine art and has participated in excavations in Turkey for the last eight years. I was encouraged from an early age to explore new subjects and modes of thought, and was exposed to diverse peoples and cultures on a regular basis. Friends of the family from around the world frequently visited our house. Even the decor of our house reflects the Middle East and Europe. When I had the chance to travel abroad, my experiences felt like an extension of the house in which I grew up. I travelled extensively throughout Europe and the Middle East. Eager to meet and exchange ideas with those I met, I actively learned foreign languages so as to better communicate and understand the countries and the peoples I was visiting. I am fluent in French and am proficient in German, Persian, and Arabic.

My curiousity about how people from foreign lands live and work also applies to people here in the United States. I have benefited greatly from the diverse experiences I have encountered in America. These many experiences have allowed me to cultivate a questioning and curious mind, and have enabled me to develop the ability to approach problems with a wide perspective. My experience as a volunteer firefighter, assistant ice hockey coach for [a day school's] varsity ice hockey team, sales coordinator for Sotheby's ..., and aircraft pilot and President and Founder of Collegiate Air Service gave me a breadth of experience not found in the "normal" college curriculum. Within the college community, I complemented my outside activities by working as Advertising Manager for *Nassau Weekly* and rowing on the Cornell and Princeton University crew teams.

One particular interest that has emerged from my background has been my interest in art. I believe that much can be understood from examining the artistic creations from a particular society. While my parents have imparted me with a strong background in the history of art and a particular understanding of the art of the Middle East, I have personally developed a fascination for American art of all periods and have a particular interest and expertise in American 18th century furniture. I derive a great deal of pleasure from this activity and find that my artistic sensibilities and art appreciation complement my other work.

My daughter's public school was suffering from a lack of leadership and enthusiasm. All but two of the eleven children in our immediate neighborhood had opted for private schools. As a PTA board member, I became aware of the principal's discouraging attitude toward his school population. When his remarks became negative toward latch-key children and Blacks, the board became motivated to seek help from the superintendent. We were able to petition the superintendent for a hearing. As a former teacher, I was asked by the board members to draft a position paper and present our allegations. As spokesperson at the hearing, I was able to convince the superintendent of the seriousness of the problem. Though the situation was a somewhat unpleasant one, the results for the community were positive. The school received a new principal. The parents became motivated. The PTA, which had never had enough money for basic supplies, undertook a campaign to fund new playground equipment. I organized an auction and we raised the $3000 necessary for our goal. My efforts in this situation demonstrate my ability to motivate others and to achieve goals.

As a high school senior, my swimming career was the focus of my life; by the time I was seventeen, I had been a world-ranked swimmer and a member of the U.S. National Team. The way I approached my swimming career very much set the pattern for the way I have approached everything since. The process of setting goals and planning strategies to achieve them, the discipline required to find the time to work out four to five hours a day while attending school full time, and the emphasis on both individual performance and team effort were all skills I developed then and have carried with me to other endeavors I have pursued. These are also skills which I think are vital to successfully pursue a career as a professional manager.

In choosing a college, I looked more closely at swimming programs than at academic programs and decided to attend the University of Southern California. Although I was very satisfied with the athletic experience at U.S.C., I began to develop interests outside the swimming pool from the first. In my second semester at college, a political science course in which I enrolled sparked an interest in academics which has grown steadily for the last seven years.

I was in the process of training for the 1980 Summer Olympics when the United States decided to boycott the Moscow Games. The boycott was pivotal for me, forcing me to look realistically at my swimming career. Recognizing that my days of amateur competition were coming to a close, I began to place much greater emphasis on my academic interests.

I chose political science as my major course of study because I felt the department would allow me to explore the widest range of fields which intrigued me. As a political science major, I was able to study philosophy, religion, economics, history and international relations, all of which helped me to develop an interdisciplinary perspective for trying to understand and analyze political and economic systems.

When graduation approached, I thought extensively about what I might want to pursue after I finished school. I considered graduate school at that point, but decided against it because as a college athlete on scholarship, I had had almost no time for anything other than my studies and swimming. Even my summers were consumed with working out and traveling to competitions, precluding almost any opportunity for a summer job. In addition to my lack of outside experience, I was not yet sure what I wanted to study on a graduate level. Although it was a difficult choice at the time, I now believe that my decision to spend some time outside of an academic setting was ultimately essential to defining my professional and academic goals.

While working at a local Credit Union, I applied for a Henry Luce Scholarship which provided for a year's residence in an Asian country of the scholar's choosing. I was attracted to the Luce program by the fact that scholars were placed in professional positions; academic appointments were discouraged. When the Luce Foundation selected me as a 1983-84 Scholar, I chose to work with the Seoul Olympic Organizing Committee (SLOOC), the organization preparing for the 1988 Seoul Olympic Games. I hoped the position would combine my interest in politics and international relations with my lifelong love for and involvement in amateur sports.

Although my choice of a country of residence had been secondary to my desire to work with SLOOC, living in Korea proved to be doubly fascinating for me. In Korea, where the economic and political systems are a mere forty years old, I had a chance to view first-hand the type of situation which had drawn me to study political and economic development as an undergraduate. I saw Korea as a country which embodied both the best and the worst of development along the Western model. The country evidences a thriving industrial sector built from the ashes of Japan's colonial legacy and the war with the North, but is saddled with an enormous foreign debt, currently the fourth largest among developing countries. Although there is no present danger of default, this debt may prove difficult to service if new markets are not found for Korea's expanding exports businesses. Living in Korea heightened my awareness of the duel-edged effects of many of the development programs which I had previously encountered only in an academic context.

When I returned to the U.S., I again considered applying to a graduate program. At that time, I was fairly certain that I wanted to study management, but I still felt unprepared to make the commitment which I knew it would mean for me. I was tremendously interested in understanding the economic issues facing Korea in particular and Asia in general, and I felt I had gained some insights during my year there. I was also very satisfied with the professional experience I had working with the SLOOC. However, I decided that to pursue my interest in economic development, I needed to gain an understanding of finance and business before returning to school. Towards that end, I went to New York in July 1985 and began a two year tenure with [an investment bank].

I am currently working in the analyst program, a two year position which provides for an intensive on-the-job experience in investment banking. I work in the financial institutions unit of the Mergers and Acquisitions department. I have been involved in a variety of projects which have included acquisitions, divestitures, and defense and consulting assignments. I feel very comfortable performing financial analysis on companies and conducting spreadsheet analysis exploring different options companies might have in terms of financing opportunities, acquisitions, and restructurings.

I have learned a great deal from my experience at [this company]. Professionally, I have had extensive client contact and have been given an incredible amount of responsibility for someone of my age and experience. While I have found my experience on Wall Street very challenging, I know that my interest still lies in the area of economic development or more specifically in the way government and business can work together to spur economic development.

Looking back on what I did at U.S.C. and what I have done since then, I believe that I have built on each experience so that I would have more to offer and bring to as well as receive from the next. I had a very broadening experience as an undergraduate where I was exposed to many different academic disciplines and picked up and refined the tools necessary to understand them better. In Asia as a Luce Scholar, I was able to look closer at some of the areas which most intrigued me in a setting outside of a university, and as an investment banker in New York, I was exposed to the world of high finance and given an intensive introduction into analyzing businesses and making strategic decisions. The ability to learn from and build on past experiences while remaining open to new ideas and new experiences is vital for anyone pursuing a career as a professional manager. I think I have been able to do this and hope to enter a graduate program where I will be able to bring my varied experiences together to the advantage of myself and the program I attend.

If my personality is a continuously evolving sculpture, my parents' divorce wet the clay and three activities molded the basic structure. My parents' divorce created a confused, introspective child determined to prove himself. Working with these basic traits, religion, music, and athletics shaped my personality. Religion propelled me most to search for new thoughts. Playing the piano I discovered the excitement inspired by an insurmountable challenge and experienced the dynamics of a group experience. Rowing crew I tested my determination and strengthened my conviction that the most satisfying achievements result from team efforts. These three activities all had a significant impact on shaping my personality. Today, I am a determined, team-oriented individual who requires a constant challenge and seeks a diversity of ideas.

My parents separated when I was seven years old. At that age, the egocentric mind of a child attempts to explain the world in terms of himself. Somehow, I felt, I must have been an instigator of the irreconcilable problems between my parents. I could not otherwise understand how two people that I loved could not love each other. Confused about people's emotions, I distanced myself from my classmates and became introverted. Meanwhile, I was determined to reestablish the love that I thought I had marred with my parent's divorce. My mother's passion was religion; my father's was music. I assumed these two interests, probably expecting to reestablish my parents' love for each other. Of course, I did not realize how important these activities would become for my self-development.

Seeing the fervor with which my mother followed Catholicism, I eagerly explored many aspects of the faith. I was a devout Catholic. However, living in a very Jewish neighborhood, I was intrigued that many people happily espoused a different religion. My parents encouraged my curiosity, and occasionally I visited Hebrew School with my Jewish friends.

These afternoon visits left me perplexed about the disparity in beliefs. As I grew older, I launched into a study of philosophies to discover the presumptuous adolescent "truth." My search uncovered ideas I had never conceived of through Nietzsche, Buddhism, Sartre, and Zen. While clinging to my Catholic heritage, I could not resolve the potpourri of persuasive ideas I had encountered.

I spent my last two years of high school at Phillips Academy where I became actively involved in the school's Catholic organization, the Newman Club. The diversity of the student body and openness of the campus priest provided the final catalyst for me to develop a personal Christian religion. While earlier I had intellectualized religion, seeking a "right" answer, I now recognized there was no absolute right nor eternal wrong: no "best" way. There are only increasingly better ways, and these better ways are often realized through a synthesis of different approaches. Senior year, as president of the Newman Club, I was consulted by classmates to discuss problems or dilemmas. We discovered solutions together through honest appraisals of the alternatives, without depending on a prefabricated morality. Solutions are not easy without rigid, determined guidelines, but what may resolve one problem may merely aggravate another. Through religion I recognized the lack of absolutism, thereby establishing a need for fresh ideas and an open mind.

I started playing the piano at age eight and became serious about music at age thirteen, when I finally began to feel the music I was playing. Practicing for hours, I would revel in the mathematical precision of a Bach fugue or the wistful ardor of a Chopin nocturne. I felt excitement when a piece took form after weeks of labor, although I understood how much more could still be expressed by the notes. Music offered an exciting challenge that required dedication and provided a thrilling sense of satisfaction.

My musical interest expanded beyond solo performance with the discovery of chamber music, a new aspect of music. Flowing from the different players of an ensemble, a chamber music piece would establishes its own will. Although each participant maintains his personality, all the members of the group work together, playing off each other, defining each other. This was the first time that I worked so closely with people. As a soloist one may admire or respect a different interpretation of a piece while maintaining an independent view. However, in chamber music the energies of the different ideas are incorporated into one body to inspire a piece with vitality. Chamber music sparked my interest in team-oriented goals.

Although I attended Yale largely because of its School of Music, as a freshman I realized that I did not have sufficient talent to establish a successful career in music. Yale had attracted pianists much more gifted than I. While I continued studying the piano throughout college and playing chamber music with friends, I decided to attempt a new challenge. I had never been athletic, but I wanted to participate on a collegiate team. I tried out for the Lightweight Crew. Although crew was known for intense physical demands, I also viewed it as an ultimate team sport.

Initially, the trial was not too difficult. We spent the afternoons practicing technique, only occasionally exerting ourselves. After Thanksgiving, we moved indoors, and the real test began. As intense workouts drove us to exhaustion, hopefuls dropped out. As teammates motivated each other through long practices, friendships formed among the survivors.

The crew became a team during Spring training in Florida. For two weeks we lived rowing. Although we competed for the same seats, comaraderie reached new highs. We all respected and trusted each other after the long trial period. Once the boats were set, the trust, loyalty and friendships consolidated during Florida would be critical for the success of the crew. During a race, when exhaustion and pain set in, testing my physical limitations, I continued knowing that my teammates were also pushing their hardest, also exhausted. We counted on each other, giving the most that we could give for ourselves and for the team. Through crew I learned how to depend on others and have others depend on me. At the end of Freshman year I received the first boat's MVP award, not for extraordinary physical prowess, but for spirit and determination. This award symbolized the rewards of everlasting friendships and self-confidence which a team sport offers.

Music and crew have imbued me with a love of challenges and taught me patience, determination, and the importance and satisfaction of working with people towards a common goal. Combining these qualities with a dynamic personal religion that leaves me restlessly searching for new ideas, I am still exploring myself and the world around me. My self-development is not over; the sculpture is far from complete.

My most enjoyable hobbies are acting and learning foreign languages. Although the two may seem quite unrelated, for me, acting and learning languages go hand in hand. Acting is a means of expression, and in certain cases an emotional outlet. Its limitations are practically nonexistent. The hours of practice, frustration and criticism which are inherent in a successful show are fully compensated by the thrill of opening night, the applause of the audience and the satisfaction of a job well done. Acting has been the major factor in developing the creative and imaginative aspect of my personality. I have been careful not to accept parts which would type cast me as a certain style of actress, for I honestly believe that I have the potential to portray a variety of characters.

Learning languages for most students is merely an academic pursuit. Although I first began to pursue foreign languages with a purely academic interest, perfecting these languages has since developed into one of my most time consuming hobbies to which I am truly devoted. My acting abilities have facilitated and enhanced the classroom and learning experience. I have found that in many elementary language courses, it is effective to act out a situation in order to better comprehend the meaning and use of certain vocabulary words. Also, in upper level literature courses, it is often useful to read aloud a section of the literature in order to visualize certain expressions inherent to the language. My fervent love for acting has rendered learning and perfecting foreign languages an entertaining pursuit and an even more enjoyable hobby.

Off-Beat Essays

As the title to this final section implies, these essays were very hard to fit into any one category. All of them, however, combine good writing, creativity, and a sense of vigor which is fun to read and meaningful.

The main problem with off-beat essays is that they can become gimmicky. High school seniors can sometimes get away with a weird application essay; business school applicants never can. An applicant almost never recovers from an essay regarded as immature and silly, so be extremely careful with your off-beat idea. Note that the essays in this group used humor only to emphasize the more serious aspects of the writer's personality and goals.

The first essay begins like a novel or a travelogue. By bringing us into the jungle, the writer captures our imagination and dramatizes the importance of her ecological interests. Her job in the New York Sanitation Department—a yawn at first glance—becomes part of an exciting theme.

The next essay describes the applicant in a light-hearted dialogue between admissions officers. By pre-empting potential criticism in an amusing manner, the writer builds his case without defensively lecturing or listing—two common mistakes.

The "retirement speech" shows far-sightedness and ambition, and the minority essay tackles a ticklish controversy head on. Displaying an admirable breadth of knowledge, the final applicant uses Buddhism, physics, psychology, and literature to introduce his work on HMO's.

Admissions officers say they don't "necessarily" want to be entertained by essays. But if you can give an experience or an idea a delightful twist, if you can demonstrate an ability to see things with a unique perspective, then your readers will go right along with you. After all, they're only human.

Red and blue macaws screeched across the sky. Monkeys chattered as they passed from tree to tree. A seven foot poisonous snake sunned itself on a branch at the river's edge. Thousands of leaf-cutter ants, each carrying a leaf ten times its size, formed a trail six inches wide.

During a river trip down a tributary of the Amazon last summer, I was awed by the natural bounty of Ecuador's tropical rain forest. The spectacular scenery was surpassed only by the diversity of species. According to some estimates, the Amazon Basin contains six million different plants, animals and insects, only a small fraction of which have been discovered and classified by scientists. Biologists, fearful that many species will disappear before they can be identified, have stepped up efforts to study them.

While western science is just beginning to comprehend the value of the tropical rain forest as a resource, the indigenous people have always found it rich in useful materials. Our guide sliced a piece of bark off a tree and explained that the Aucas used its slippery underside as a lubricant to dislodge canoes stuck on sand. He directed us to another tree which produced a substance used to heal wounds, one of 1300 medicinal plants known to the Indians of the Amazon.

Biological diversity in the tropical forest stems from the complexity of its ecosystem. After having us taste the lemon ants crawling inside a hollow branch of a nearby tree, our guide explained that the ants and the tree were interdependent. The tree provides the ants with a home and a source of food; the ants protect the tree from natural predators. Both have evolved in such a way that neither can live without the other. This pattern of symbiosis is repeated throughout the jungle, creating a diverse yet fragile environment.

Because of this fragility, it does not take much to upset the delicate natural balance of the tropical forest. Our guide told us that in six months the landscape before us would be changed forever. Ecuador's government, already pumping 210,000 gallons of oil out of the jungle every month, planned to expand production to improve the country's financial situation. The proposed new wells would encroach on the rapidly shrinking boundaries of the virgin forest. The noise from the heavy machinery alone would drive the animals from the region completely.

I could empathize with the reasons behind the government's decision to exploit the tropical forest's short-term potential. My travels around Ecuador made me acutely aware of the need to generate capital and raise the standard of living of its people. Even if Ecuador recognized the long-term value of preserving the tropical forest, it could not afford to lose present oil revenue. In Quito, I watched students go on strike when the bus fare went up from 2 to 3 cents. In the Andean highlands, I visited villages which had no potable water and infant mortality rates of eighty-five percent. At this time, the tropical forest's raw materials provide Ecuador with its best hope for a brighter economic future.

Unfortunately, many of the tropical forest's resources are non-renewable and their disappearance will have serious global consequences. Each year, 25,000 square miles of tropical forests are cleared by developing countries worldwide. In the process, thousands of species are lost. This translates into the greatest rate of species extinction since the dinosaurs vanished from the earth 65 million years ago. We cannot begin to calculate the loss because we do not know exactly what we are losing. What we do know is that the tropical forest has produced drugs to treat Hodgkin's disease and leukemia, germoplasm to revitalize crops, and the most prolific plant foods on earth.

Tropical forests face destruction because they are under-valued as resources. The international scientific community, which vocally supports the preservation of the earth's biological diversity, has only recently recast the plight of the rain forest in economic terms. Biologists now argue that the study of unknown plants and animals of the tropical forest will lead to agricultural and pharmaceutical applications to benefit all humankind. It is in our self-interest to preserve the earth's tropical forests and it is our responsibility to ensure their biological diversity. We have to begin to think about tropical forests in new ways.

Changing the way society values a resource is a difficult task. People often have to feel the direct impact of a crisis to alter their behavior. As an undergraduate, I encountered this in my study of the New Haven water supply at the turn of the century. Although the health risks of impure water were known and the technological means of purification had been developed, the people of New Haven did not demand filtration of their water supply until a typhoid epidemic claimed the lives of 51 residents. Only after New Haven experienced the tragedy of water-borne disease first hand were its citizens willing to pay the price of keeping their water pure.

People tend to respond resoundingly in the face of a crisis. Unfortunately, if we must wait until people feel the direct impact of the tropical forest's disappearance, there will not be much left to save. Nevertheless, my experience has shown me that there are other ways to make people change their behavior.

Only a short while ago, few people considered the Fresh Kills waste disposal site on Staten Island in New York City a resource, let alone a valuable commodity. The price to dump at the landfill was low, reflecting its perceived worth. No attempt was made to regulate the volume of New York City's waste. Some city managers recognized that Fresh Kills had a finite capacity and that other landfill sites or methods of disposal would have to be found. They proposed a technological solution: building resource recovery plants to burn garbage for energy. What these city managers did not foresee was the public resistance to the plants they intended to build. Nor did they anticipate the scope of the problem.

Throughout the Northeast, as environmental regulations have grown more stringent and the value of land has increased, towns and cities have run out of places to put their garbage. Few have developed replacement facilities such as resource recovery plants or have significantly reduced the volume of their waste through recycling. Therefore, they have had to pay steep prices to export their garbage to available landfills in distant counties and states. Unless these municipalities develop innovative solutions to their waste disposal problems, the situation will only get worse.

Many towns and cities in the Northeast face garbage crises because they have failed to assign the appropriate cost to waste disposal. As an analyst for the New York City Department of Sanitation, I am helping the City attempt to avoid the same mistakes by changing its waste disposal pricing policies while the City still has landfill space. We use an economic model to capture the present and future costs of operating New York City's entire waste disposal system and we base our rates on marginal pricing principles. These principles use the highest cost facility in the system to define the base rate. These rates set an efficient price for disposal, encourage recycling and provide incentives to private industry to develop new methods of waste disposal.

Although we have generated over 60 million dollars in annual revenue through dump fees, we have not yet realized our goal of diverting tonnage from the landfill. We have failed for a variety of reasons. In spite of the fact that we have raised our fees to unprecedented levels, we still charge rates at our landfill which fall below the true cost of waste disposal. My economic analysis dictates that we immediately raise our rates to reflect the cost of disposing the last ton. We have instead adopted a more gradual price increase to avoid shocking the system and give the commercial waste haulers some time to adjust to our new strategy. Furthermore, the money generated by dump fees goes into the City's general fund. If this money were earmarked to develop markets for recycled products, we might experience reductions in tonnage. The political considerations which have kept our rates artificially low and diverted money from recycling have cost the City valuable landfill space.

New York City's attempt to use price to preserve its landfill space provides a useful tool to examine the management of natural resources. There may be lessons for Ecuador in New York's experience. Marginal pricing which assigns depletion costs to non-renewable uses of resources could theoretically preserve the tropical forest. It could also pay for the costs of preservation by generating revenue from an international base of users such as pharmaceutical and chemical companies who benefit directly from the forest's products. Marginal pricing offers no guarantee that the tropical forest, like New York City's remaining landfill, will be preserved but, accompanied by political commitment, it promises some real hope.

My experience in city government has given me insight into methods to preserve natural resources. It has also shown me that successful policy cannot be sustained on the basis of correct analysis alone. Decision-makers must be guided by political will and vision. My goal is to achieve a position in which I can take the lead in determining how natural resources are allocated based on respect for the environment, sound economics, and an awareness of future consequences.

To answer UCLA's direction to "Write your own essay question and answer it. Take a risk", one candidate did the following:

How would Bob and Jane, two esteemed members of the UCLA Admissions staff, discuss MBA candidate Bill Johnson's application for admission? Bob is against admission. Jane wants to accept him. (Any resemblence to actual persons or events is purely coincidental and should not be held against the applicant.)

    Bob: O.K. Jane, I've looked at Johnson's file and frankly, I've got my doubts.
    Jane: Bob, get serious. We've got to accept this kid. Give me specifics—if you don't want him, tell me exactly why.
    Bob: For starters, his GMAT score is mediocre.*
    Jane: You think a silly test tells you anything about anybody? Johnson's always tested very averagely. Andover and Princeton accepted him despite his mediocre SSAT and SAT scores. I mean a 560/620 on the SAT must be 200 or so points below the Princeton average. Yet look at his academic record there: graduated cum laude in history, got an A- on a unique Senior Thesis, and received A's on his Junior Independent work. This is a very bright kid.
    Bob: Alright, but he's a little young; he doesn't have enough experience to really take advantage of our program.

Jane: I was just about to get to that. Do you want pizza or Chinese tonight? Pizza? Good. At least we can agree on something. Call up Domino's while I lecture you on Johnson's experience. He's written advertisements that have appeared in *Time, Esquire,* and *Glamour* among other national publications. He supervised a direct mail operation that raised $2,000,000. The Zschau campaign was the largest federal election campaign in the United States in 1986, the second most expensive in the history of the country and Johnson was a part of it. On the campaign, he was given goals and he exceeded them; he's met deadlines, knows how to communicate to a variety of markets across the country, understands budgets and has worked carefully with numbers. Direct mail is dependent on accurate interpretation of the returns, so that you can predict things like yield, rate per piece mailed, cost per piece mailed... so that you can learn how often to mail and to whom. I think he's done an awful lot in a short amount of time.

Bob: I don't know, doesn't seem like he's taken any risks.

Jane: You've got no case here. As most of his Princeton pals were interviewing for jobs on Wall Street, Johnson took a chance and moved to California. I think that shows a lot of initiative—I mean, all of his friends, his family, were in the East. When he joined the campaign in February 1986, Ed Zschau didn't even register in the polls. Either Johnson was crazy or he seized upon a unique opportunity. I subscribe to the latter.

Bob: Well, I subscribe to magazines.

Jane: Admit it, we should let him in—he's a go-getter, he's smart, his recommendations are strong, he's motivated and he's had unique and solid experiences. Oh good, the pizza arrived.

Bob: Ahhh... mushrooms and pepperoni.

Jane: You know I hate mushrooms.

Bob: Yup.

*This is an assumption. I took the test on January 24, 1987.

The topic: "Write your retirement speech." Here's how one applicant handled it:

Members of Congress, distinguished guests, ladies and gentlemen, members of the press, I thank you for spending an evening seeing this old codger off. Now that the coffee is poured, sit back and endure the reminiscings of a man about to spend three months sailing on a boat no larger than the cubicle assigned him in his first job as analyst at an investment bank called Salomon Brothers. (You know it better as the merchant bank Salomon, Sumitomo and Sons.) Well, there have been more offices than I dare count since then. But throughout my career, if there was one thing I could count on, it has been the continuing internationalization of the world's economy. I suppose that's why I've had so many offices!

Shuttling between private industry, supranational agencies and government positions—as I and most of you here have done—is a requirement of a world where few transactions fail to touch all three of these sectors. Before assuming my present position in the State Department, I was, as you know, managing partner of an international economic consulting firm. Our firm encountered numerous companies—in both service and manufacturing—that failed financially because they dealt ineffectively with (or worse, ignored) one or more of these cornerstones of the world's economy.

Now I never thought I'd learn Korean, or wine and dine

government bureaucrats in Eastern Mongolia, or prepare an annual report in North American Currency Units—but I've done it all and more these past thirty years. In fact, the three examples I just gave were all required to complete a series of manufacturing and trade agreements for a supra-tech company I used to manage. I arranged for one of our products—designed by my company here in the States—to be manufactured in Mongolia and imported through a Korean import-export firm to the ever-growing markets of that country. All parties demanded that company financials be reported in the common language of NACUs. I complied with many (but not all) requests and signed agreements that still provide profits for everyone involved.

If asked to put my finger on the reason why I have been successful at working with and in such varied institutional and economic climates, I'd say I was fortunate in having a strong educational foundation from which to launch my career. A small liberal arts college in Massachusetts and a larger business school farther inland provided that foundation by instilling in me the necessity of adapting one's strategy to different environments—whether when reading a novel by Joseph Conrad or analyzing the economy of a third-world nation. Few situations render themselves accessible to standard strategies. Besides, who can agree on what constitutes these standard strategies?

Well, we can all probably agree on what constitutes a too-long speech so I'll close with an invitation to any of you sailors here tonight to sail along with me for a spell and chat some more about these and future times.

When I served on the U.C.'s admissions committee, I justified special treatment for minorities by identifying the special, but not easily quantifiable, disadvantages that minorities have in relation to the majority white population. Nevertheless, though I am Asian, and would therefore qualify for special consideration in some programs, I prefer to be chosen on my qualifications, without reference to ethnic status. My skills and experience alone qualify me for the GSM.

Like most Asians, I'm sensitive to others' needs. I listen to others carefully, and consider their opinions seriously. When necessary, I will sacrifice my needs for the benefit of others. I like to think of myself as a bamboo person: willing to bend to strong winds—but I do not break. (A suitable analogy for Japanese-Americans, I believe.)

Like most Asian-Americans, I have demonstrated high academic achievement, with strong undergraduate and graduate grade point averages in challenging classes. Like most Asians, I'm competitive. I've become a competitive runner, even though I began running only two years ago. (I now compete with people who have been running at least seven years.)

What distinguishes me from other Asians is my leadership skills and experience. Most of my friends are happy being technicians, but they are confused by the interpersonal and organizational aspects of jobs and professional relationships. Perhaps most Asians are satisfied with being experts or technicians, but not I. I want to be *an expert and a manager*. This requires being introverted—to focus on complex ideas and research; and it requires being extroverted—to manage other people, to bring experts together, and to create agreement which promotes changes.

My past leadership roles make me different from most Asians. My community work for U.C., Common Cause, and Proposition 14 demonstrates my leadership ability. But even my work at RAND demonstrates leadership. I was hired to be a technician—an evaluator, experimental designer, and instrument developer—but in fact I have become the project leader of field research. Not only do I develop and evaluate the tutor, but I coordinate the work of others.

Unlike most Asians, I understand American culture. I know its politics, psychology, and emotions. I'm not inhibited by being Japanese or being different. I participate in the community completely. Nor am I angry about the position of Asians in American society. I am accepting, though certainly not passive. I work with people of other backgrounds, showing them my culture and learning about theirs. Moreover, I have better interpersonal and verbal skills than most Asians. (Because of my strong verbal skills, I am often encouraged to do a lot of writing in my job, and I work extensively with writers in the UCLA English Department.) And finally, unlike most Asians, I understand myself. There are complexities which most Asians in America do not understand about themselves. Asian and American cultures differ in ethics, values, measures of success, and personal relationships. I have spent much time thinking about these conflicts, and I have resolved many of the personal struggles which undermine Asian-Americans.

W hen I was seven years old I wanted to be an astronaut. Since that time, my interests have followed a broad yet related set of disciplines, including physics, philosophy, psychology and management consulting. Currently, I plan to pursue a career in health care management. I believe the diverse nature of my interests and experiences is a distinguishing asset in my candidacy for business school.

Wanting to be an astronaut reflected a childhood desire to participate in some dramatic way in human exploration. This yearning for space travel matured over time into a fascination for physics, particularly atomic physics. During two summers in high school I worked as a research assistant in the University of Washington Nuclear Physics Laboratory, the youngest person ever to hold that position. The study of physics trained me to think both quantitatively and conceptually. In struggling to understand the full scope of modern physics I discovered a tangential literature relating the principles of Western physics to those of Eastern philosophy. A striking similarity exists between relativity theory and Oriental mysticism. Both reject Newtonian "logic" as an adequate means of conceptualizing the physical universe, while stressing the essential interconnection of the observer and the observed. This discovery had a profound effect on my intellectual development. As my fascination with philosophy grew, my corresponding interest in physics waned. While a senior in high school I traveled alone to Nepal to study Buddhism. During this period I became especially intrigued by the question of man's nature. What most distinguishes Eastern and Western philosophies is their concept of self. Buddhism argues that man's notion of self identity is a fallacy perpetuated by his insecurity about his own mortality. In pursuing the issue I grew frustrated by philosophy's inability to establish anything concrete about man's nature. To advance my understanding I needed a mental discipline with more of an empirical base. Psychology was the obvious choice.

As a psychology major at Yale University I explored the full spectrum of departmental course offerings. My studies covered not only the philosophical implications of psychology, but the biological ones as well. By the end of my tenure as an undergraduate I narrowed my field of interest to organizational behavior. The study of organizations excited me because of its broader relevance outside the world of academia. In a senior essay, I examined the relationship between job satisfaction and absenteeism. Reviewing over 100 studies on the subject, I developed a unique way of interpreting disparate results. Traditional theories claim that higher job satisfaction lowers absenteeism. Studies on the issue typically attempt to statistically verify the presence of a correlation. Equal volumes of literature "prove" and "disprove" the theory. What researchers uniformally overlooked was the inability of correlational research to determine causality. In companies where a structure exists to reward good attendance, lower absenteeism may actually cause increased job satisfaction. Where this structure fails to exist it also seems to explain the lack of a correlation.

My college studies of organizational behavior inspired me to seek some way of pursuing management professionally. I had explored management consulting the summer before my senior year by working for a general consulting firm in Seattle and the experience had been extremely positive. Consulting provided a way to pursue my general interest in management while sampling a broad range of business problem solving situations. After graduating from Yale, I chose a job with ... a consulting firm specializing in the health care industry. The managing and financing of health care in this country were on the verge of an unparalleled transformation. For this reason I perceived health care to be an especially dynamic arena for consulting.

While at [work] I have worked on projects in a number of

health care sectors. For a suburban teaching hospital in
Chicago our firm did a series of studies directed at implement-
ing product line management to increase market share. The
project began with an evaluation of the impact of area-wide
utilization declines on our client's competitive position in each
of its principle markets. For this phase of the project, I
developed a computer model to assess how various market and
population trends would affect the hospital's census. Using
these projections we determined which of the hospital's inpa-
tient services would make the most promising candidates for a
shift to product line management. The first service selected
was Obstetrics. Having made this determination, we conducted
extensive consumer research to discover what program en-
hancements were necessary and how best to market the product. This phase of the work included focus groups of area
residents, clandestine visits to local competitors, and research
into national "birth market" trends. I participated in all
aspects of this work, including a considerable amount of time
working directly with the client.

Currently I am working on the development of a Health
Maintenance Organization (HMO) for a major academic
medical center in Manhattan. HMO market penetration in New
York City is now approximately 11%. By 1990 that figure is ex-
pected to triple. Faced with this market scenario, our client
contracted [us] to assess the desirability of a university hospital
creating its own HMO. Our initial feasibility study examined
the track record of other medical school sponsored HMOs, the
market feasibility of sponsoring such an HMO in New York City, and the probability of financial success. I was responsible
for the bulk of this research, including a series of interviews
with area benefit managers to assess their receptivity. As a
result of this work, the Board of Governors of the hospital has
given its initial endorsment to develop an HMO. At the present
time, we are researching program structure alternatives and
possible joint venture partners. The target for initial operations
is January 1987.

The last 18 months of employment have shaped my professional aspirations in two fundamental ways. I have decided
that I want to get out of management consulting but that I
want to pursue a career in health care management. By actually working in a consulting capacity I have discovered how

frustrating it is not to be able to manage directly. A consultants role is inherently limited by his outside status. The very objectivity which makes consultants valuable limits the amount of emotional commitment they can invest in the business problems they face. At the same time, the more I have learned about health care the more fascinated I have become by the field. An industry representing 11% of GNP is undergoing a complete financial transformation. If this change is managed successfully the result will be significantly improved health care for every stratum of society at a lower cost to society overall. It's an exciting prospect, and one I want to participate in.

Some Final Advice
from *Business Week*

Though this article from Business Week doesn't really say anything we haven't already said, we thought it clearly and succinctly summarized the points we have tried to make in this book.

One Key to B-School: Your Essay

To write a succinct description of how you handled a real-life ethical dilemma can be a real challenge. So can describing the details of a failure in your career.

But if you try to enroll as an MBA candidate at Harvard, Stanford, or any top B-school, you'll have to meet such challenges. Satisfying a school's academic criteria is just one hurdle. Another is impressing the admissions staff with written responses to a series of questions designed to reveal the real you. How can you create a good impression?

Admissions officers say that most applications sound monotonously alike. Your essays should show how different you are, not how great you are. To stand out among countless applicants who all work capably at their jobs, tell how you have tutored underprivileged children. Discuss your Uncle Scrooge comics collection or your role as a guitarist in a rock band or cellist in a classical quartet.

"We pay a lot of attention to what people say about their lives outside the classroom or office," says Alice Brookner, associate director of admissions for the University of Chicago's B-school.

Accomplishments count, but schools also want to assess your values. So discuss an acomplishment in terms of the obstacles you overcame to achieve it.

No Rambling. Don't plan to knock off the essays in an evening. Completing a set will take 20 to 40 hours. On each one, stick to the point you want to make. For an idea of what to emphasize, look over the school's brochures: They often contain clues about what kinds of students are wanted. Those with managerial potential? Diversified skills? Play up how well you fit their bill.

"Most candidates tend to use a grab-bag approach, hoping they'll hit on something that clicks with us," complains Stephen Christakos, Wharton's director of admissions. "We don't want people to ramble on."

Honesty is vital. "Don't play games," advises Karen Page, who runs a Learning Annex seminar for MBA applicants in New York. "Play up everything you've done for what it's worth, but don't cross the line to lie or cheat."

If you know a graduate of the school, ask him or her to read your essays before you turn them in. What about attention-getting ploys like writing in crayon or sending a videotape? Some applicants are bold enough to try them. But, as a rule, "we really don't like gimmicks," says Bruce Paton, director of admissions at Stanford.   —*John A. Byrne*

About the Authors

Boykin Curry and Brian Kasbar, who grew up together in Summit, New Jersey, are members of the Yale Class of 1988. Their first book, *Essays That Worked* (for college applications), was an immediate hit, appearing on bestseller lists and receiving wide critical acclaim. They both plan to pursue entrepreneurial careers when they graduate.

More Great Books
from Mustang Publishing

Europe for Free by Brian Butler. If you think a trip to Europe is just one long exercise in cashing traveler's checks, then this is the book for you. The author describes *thousands* of activities, sights, and other fun things to see and do—and nothing costs one single lira, franc, or pfennig. *"An excellent guide no matter what your budget"—International Living.* **$9.95**

Europe: Where the Fun Is by Rollin Riggs & Bruce Jacobsen. No hotels, no museums, no historic sights. Just the wildest bars, the coolest nightclubs, the hottest beaches, the weirdest flea markets—just the fun stuff, in all the major cities of Europe. A terrific supplement to the major guidebooks. *Named one of the 25 best European travel guides by "Changing Times" magazine.* **$8.95**

Essays That Worked: 50 Essays from Successful Applications to the Nation's Top Colleges by Boykin Curry & Brian Kasbar. Applying to college? Dread the essay? This book can help. With 50 outstanding essays from schools like Yale, Duke, and Wesleyan—plus lots of helpful advice from admissions officers—this book will inspire any college applicant. *"50 admissions essays, each one a winner"—New York Times.* **$8.95**

The Student's Guide to the Best Summer Jobs in Alaska by Josh Groves. Thousands of young adults head for Alaska each summer, seeking jobs in the potentially lucrative fishing industry. This book offers the most thorough information on the Alaska summer job scene available. *"Highly recommended"—The Tartan, Carnegie-Mellon Univ.* **$7.95**

The Complete Book of Beer Drinking Games by Andy Griscom, Ben Rand, & Scott Johnston. Attention party animals! With 50 of the world's greatest beer games—plus lots of "really important stuff"—this book has quickly become the imbiber's bible. Over 100,000 copies sold! *"A classic in American Literature"—The Torch, St. John's Univ.* **$5.95**

Beer Games II: The Exploitative Sequel by Griscom, Rand, Johnston, & Balay. This uproarious sequel is even funnier than the original! With 30 new beer games, more hilarious articles and cartoons, and the wild Beer Catalog, this book must be seen to be believed. *"Absolutely fantastic!"—34th Street Newspaper, Univ. of Pennsylvania.* **$5.95**

Prove It All Night! The Bruce Springsteen Trivia Book by Deborah Mayer. So you think you're an expert on The Boss, eh? Well, then, answer this: Where are 10th Avenue and E Street? Whom did Bruce write *Fire* for? What Bruce songs mention the word "beer"? For the answers, you need this highly entertaining book. A great gift! *"The ultimate '80s quiz"—Associated Press.* **$5.95**

The Cathouses of Nevada: A Sensual Guide by J. R. Schwartz. Over two million people visit the legal brothels of Nevada each year, and this book has become a must for the discriminating pleasure-seeker. An opinionated, entertaining travel book. Don't go to Nevada without it! *"An essential guide"—Adam Magazine.* **$6.95**

———————————

Mustang books should be available at your local bookstore. If not, you may order directly from us. Send a check or money order for the price of the book—plus $1.00 for postage *per book* —to Mustang Publishing, P. O. Box 9327, New Haven, CT 06533. Allow three weeks for delivery.

Add $2.50 per book for delivery in one week. Connecticut residents must add 7.5% sales tax. Foreign orders: U.S. funds only, please, and add $3.00 postage per book.